Cycling Traffic Free; South East
Nick Cotton

First published 2010

ISBN 978 0 7110 3433 4

Published by Ian Allan Publishing

An imprint of Ian Allan Publishing Ltd, Hersham, Surrey KT12 4RG.
Printed in England by Ian Allan Printing Ltd, Hersham, Surrey KT12 4RG.

Visit the Ian Allan Publishing website at www.ianallanpublishing.com

Distributed in the United States of America and Canada by BookMasters Distribution Services.

Code 1004/D3

CONTENTS

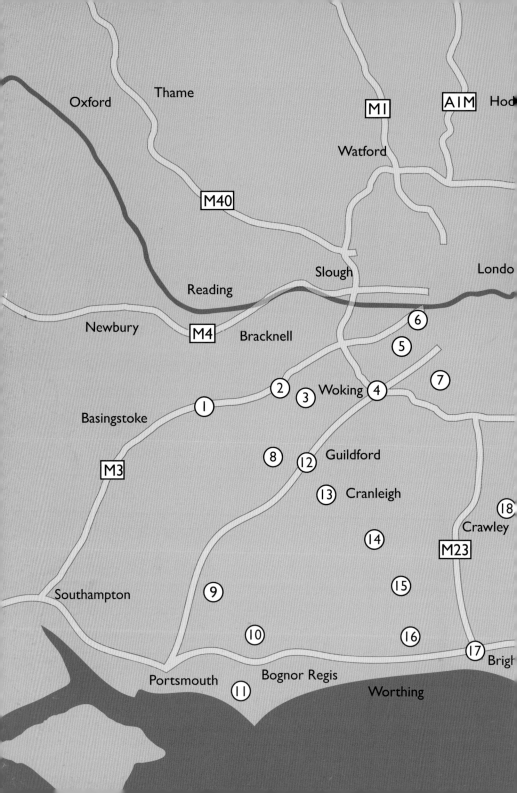

INTRODUCTION

More and more people are realising that cycling is good for both health and well-being. The government has started showing a real interest in promoting cycling as a way of solving transport problems and the National Cycle Network has had a positive effect, changing lifestyles and people's choice of transport. However, vehicle numbers are still increasing, which means that even minor lanes can become busy with traffic. You can very rarely be guaranteed to find the safety, peace and quiet that are the essential ingredients of a family bike ride on the road network.

This book describes 30 routes, many of them easy and waymarked, where you can cycle free from traffic and gives details about where to find information about other rides.

OTHER ROUTES IN BRIEF

In addition to the 30 main rides featured in the book there are several routes in the area which are worth a brief mention:

LONDON

Wandle Way

Follows the River Wandle from the River Thames at Wandsworth Bridge south to Croydon. www.merton.gov.uk/wandletrail

Waterlink Way

Runs south from the River Thames at Greenwich to South Norwood Park. www.sustrans.org.uk and put 'Waterlink Way' in the 'Search' box

Wimbledon Common

There are a limited number of tracks available for cyclists. www.wpcc.org.uk/sport.html

SURREY

Reigate Hill

There is a superb 1½-mile section on the North Downs Way to the west of the Reigate Hill car park (and cafe) with fantastic views to the south.

Norbury Park, south of Leatherhead

In many ways similar to Horton Park (Ride 7), this is a short waymarked route on good quality bridleways around a country park. www.surreywildlifetrust.co.uk and click on 'Our places' then 'Norbury Park'.

Newlands Corner, on the A25 east of Guildford

There is a good section of the North Downs Way on a broad stone track that runs east from Newlands. www.surreywildlifetrust.co.uk and click on 'Our places' then 'Newlands Corner'.

Blackwater Valley Path
A predominantly traffic-free route runs up the Blackwater Valley parallel with the A331. www.blackwater-valley.org.uk/path

SUSSEX
Hastings seafront
There is a 2-mile section of seafront promenade west from the centre of Hastings.

Rye, Camber & Lydd
There are two sections of traffic-free path running parallel with the road between Rye and Lydd (although not through Camber itself). www.kent.gov.uk > leisure-and-culture > countryside-and-coast > cycling

Chichester Canal
This can be followed for 2 miles south from Chichester railway station as far as the A286.

Devil's Dyke Railway Trail (Brighton)
A short railway path climbing from Hangleton (northwest of Hove) up onto the South Downs at Devil's Dyke.

KENT
Margate to Sandwich
The Viking Trail can be followed east then south round the Kent coast from Margate, at the end of Ride 28, through North Foreland, Broadstairs and Ramsgate to Cliffs End on a mixture of quiet roads and traffic-free paths. www.vikingcoastaltrail.co.uk

North Downs Way
The North Downs Way from Charing Hill to Hollingbourne offers a good ride on mountain bikes in the summer after a few dry days (this is not specifically a cycle trail but it is reasonably flat with a fairly good surface).

HAMPSHIRE & ISLE OF WIGHT
Isle of Wight
The island has three short railway paths (1, 2 and 3) and a longer one (4). They are:
1. Yarmouth to Freshwater Bay
2. Cowes to Newport
3. Shanklin to Wroxall
4. Sandown to Newport
The Tennyson Trail east of Freshwater Bay is a tough but beautiful bridleway ridge ride with fantastic views in all directions. www.cyclewight.org.uk

Meon Valley Trail, Wickham (north of Fareham) to East Meon

This used to be a top grade railway path but is now only suitable for mountain bikes. www3.hants.gov.uk/cycling and search 'Meon Valley Trail'.

Useful websites

More and more cycling information is being made available on the Internet and the better websites are constantly being upgraded. If you are prepared to search for 'Cycling' or 'Cycle routes' on local authority websites you will normally find details of routes and leaflets, some of which you will be able to download and print off at home.

LONDON

www.tfl.gov.uk/cycling
www.lcc.org.uk
www.royalparks.org.uk.

KENT

www.kent.gov.uk > leisure-and-culture > countryside-and-coast >cycling
www.visitkent.co.uk > Come and explore > Outdoors > Cycling

SUSSEX

www.eastsussex.gov.uk > Leisure & tourism > Cycling
www.cyclingeastsussex.co.uk
www.westsussex.gov.uk > Roads & Transport > Walking and Cycling >
Cycle Routes & Maps
www.westsussex.info/cycling.shtml
www.visitsussex.org > Things to See and Do > Walking and Cycling

SURREY

www.surreycc.gov.uk and put 'Cycle Guides' in the 'Search' box.

HAMPSHIRE

www.hants.gov.uk/cycling
www.hampshirescountryside.co.uk/site/cycling

ISLE OF WIGHT

www.cyclewight.org.uk

www.sustrans.org.uk

The Sustrans website is being improved year by year and this is often the best place to start on your hunt for cycling information relating to rides close to where you live or where you are going on holiday.

TOURIST INFORMATION CENTRES

Kent

Ashford	01233 629165
Broadstairs	08702 646 111
Canterbury	01227 378100
Cranbrook	01580 712538
Deal	01304 369 576
Dover	01304 205 108
Edenbridge	01732 865368
Faversham	01795 534 542
Folkestone	01303 258 594
Gravesend	01474 337600
Herne Bay	01227 361911
Hythe	01303 266 421
Maidstone	01622 602 169
Margate	08702 646 111
New Romney	01797 362 353
Ramsgate	08702 646 111
Rochester	01634 843 666
Sandwich	01304 613 565
Sevenoaks	01732 450 305
Swanley	01322 614 660
Tenterden	01580 763 572
Tonbridge	01732 770929
Tunbridge Wells	01892 515675
Whitstable	01227 275482

East Sussex

Battle	01424 773721
Brighton	0906 711 2255
Eastbourne	0906 711 2212
Hastings	01424 0845 274
Lewes	01273 483 448
Rye	01797 226696
Seaford	01323 897 426

West Sussex

Arundel	01903 882268
Bognor Regis	01243 823 140
Burgess Hill	01444 238 202
Chichester	01243 775888
Crawley	01293 846 968
Horsham	01403 211 661
Littlehampton	01903 721 866
Midhurst	01730 817322
Petworth	01798 343523
Worthing	01903 221 066

Surrey

Guildford	01483 444333

Hampshire

Aldershot	01252 320 968
Alton	01420 88448
Andover	01264 324320
Fareham	01329 221 342
Fordingbridge	01425 654560
Gosport	023 9252 2944
Hayling Island	023 9246 7111
Lymington	01590 689 000
Lyndhurst	023 8028 2269
Petersfield	01730 268829
Portsmouth	023 9282 6722
Ringwood	01425 470896
Romsey	01794 512 987
Southampton	023 8083 3333
Winchester	01962 840 500

WHERE TO CYCLE TRAFFIC-FREE
SOUTH OF LONDON

In general, traffic-free cycling routes can be divided into six categories:

- Dismantled railways
- Forestry Commission routes
- Waterside routes including reservoirs, canals, riverside routes and seafront promenades
- London parks and country parks
- Routes created by local authorities, often as part of the National Cycle Network
- The Rights of Way network – byways and bridleways

DISMANTLED RAILWAYS

The vast majority of Britain's railway system was built in the 50 years from 1830 to 1880. After the invention of the car and the development of the road network from the turn of the 20th century onwards, the railways went into decline and in the 1960s many of the lines were closed and the tracks lifted. This was the famous 'Beeching Axe'. It is a great tragedy that Dr Beeching was not a keen leisure cyclist! Had he set in motion the development of leisure trails along the course of the railways he was so busy closing, then we could boast one of the finest recreational cycling networks in the world.

As it is, many of the railways were sold off in small sections to adjacent landowners and the continuity of long sections of dismantled track was lost. Almost 50 years on, some local authorities have risen to the challenge and created some fine trails along the course of the dismantled railways. Within this book the Downs Link (Rides 13, 14, 15 and 16), the Centurion Way (Ride 10), the Cuckoo Trail (Ride 23), the Worth Way (Ride 18), the Forest Way (Ride 19) and the Crab & Winkle Way (Ride 29) are all good examples.

Dismantled railways make good cycle trails for two reasons. First, the gradients tend to be very gentle and second, the broad stone base is ideal for creating a smooth firm surface for bicycles.

FORESTRY COMMISSION LAND

There are four Forestry Commission holdings with waymarked routes in the area covered by this book:

1. Alice Holt Forest, southwest of Farnham (Route 8)
2. Queen Elizabeth Country Park, south of Petersfield (Route 9)
3. Friston Forest, west of Eastbourne (Route 24)
4. Bedgebury Forest, southwest of Cranbrook (Route 22)

There are also many smaller woodlands where it is easy to devise your own routes (for example, Kings Wood, southwest of Canterbury or West Walk, north of Fareham). The Forestry Commission website www.forestry.gov.uk is an excellent source of information about cycling and mountain biking.

WATERSIDE ROUTES: CANAL TOWPATHS, RIVERSIDE ROUTES, RESERVOIRS AND SEAFRONT PROMENADES

The British Waterways Board undertook a national survey of its 2,000 miles of towpath to see what percentage was suitable for cycling. Unfortunately, the results were not very encouraging – only about 10% meet the specified requirements. The rest are too narrow, too rutted, too overgrown or pass under too many low bridges. In certain cases regional water boards have co-ordinated with local authorities to improve the towpaths for all users. It is to be hoped that this collaboration continues and extends throughout the country.

Cycling along canal towpaths can provide plenty of interest – wildlife, barges and locks – and the gradient tends to be flat. However, even the best-quality towpaths are not places to cycle fast as they are often busy with anglers and walkers and it is rare that cycling two abreast is feasible. For more information go to the British Waterways website at www.waterscape.com.

The most important waterways for cycling in the area covered by the book are the River Thames (Rides 5 and 30), the Basingstoke Canal (Rides 1, 2 and 3) and the Wey Navigation (Rides 4 and 12). Other waterways in the South East such as the Kennet & Avon Canal, the Grand Union Canal and the Lee & Stort Navigation are covered in another book in the series: *Cycling Traffic Free: Home Counties.*

Bewl Water (Ride 21) is one of the few reservoirs in the South East with a cycle trail around it. There are seafront promenades in Brighton (Ride 17), Hythe (Ride 25), Deal (Ride 27) and Margate (Ride 28).

LONDON PARKS AND COUNTRY PARKS

Several parks in London have cycle trails – see www.royalparks.org.uk. The Tamsin Trail around Richmond Park is included here (Ride 6); there are a limited amount of trails on Wimbledon Common. Country parks with routes include Horton Park near Epsom (Ride 7) and Norbury Park near Leatherhead (see 'Other Routes in Brief').

ROUTES CREATED BY LOCAL AUTHORITIES

By using a mixture of quiet lanes and improved footpaths and bridleways local authorities can signpost and promote a route to make the most of existing networks. These include the Salterns Way south of Chichester (Ride 11), the trail from Tonbridge Castle to Penshurst Place (Ride 20) and the cliff top ride between Folkestone and Dover (Ride 26).

RIGHTS OF WAY NETWORK: THE SOUTH DOWNS WAY AND THE NORTH DOWNS WAY

The South Downs Way is a bridleway along its entire length and offers tough challenges for fit cyclists on mountain bikes. It runs for 100 miles from Winchester to Eastbourne with many thousands of feet of climbing. There are several easier sections where you can drive to a car park at the top of the ridge and explore the trail for a short distance either side of the starting point, maintaining height and enjoying magnificent views out to the English Channel and down into the Sussex Weald. These rides are tougher than those along railway paths and canal towpaths

and should only be undertaken on mountain bikes (preferably with suspension) after a few dry days in summer. Suggested rides are:

1. Kithurst Hill & Rackham Hill southwest of Storrington (northwest of Worthing)
2. Near to Chanctonbury Ring, west of Steyning (north of Worthing)
3. Ditchling Beacon, north of Brighton
4. Firle Beacon, southeast of Lewes

Running from Farnham to Canterbury, the North Downs Way is at times a byway or bridleway (where you can legally ride) but for much of its length is a footpath and cycling is *not* allowed. The best sections for cycling are:

1. East from Newlands Corner, near Guildford
2. Near Reigate Hill
3. From Charing Hill to Hollingbourne northwest of Ashford

OTHER CYCLE ROUTES

If you wish to venture beyond the relatively protected world of cycle trails, there are three choices: buy a guidebook covering mountain bike rides or rides on the lane network, look on websites for leaflets produced by local authorities or devise your own route.

Should you choose the third option, study the relevant Ordnance Survey Landranger map: the yellow roads criss-crossing the countryside represent the smaller quieter lanes. When cycling off-road you must stay on legal rights of way: it is illegal to cycle on footpaths, but you are allowed to use bridleways, byways open to all traffic (BOATs) and roads used as public paths (RUPPs). These are all marked on Ordnance Survey maps.

Devising routes 'blind' can sometimes be a bit of a hit-or-miss affair, however. Some tracks may turn out to be very muddy and overgrown or no more than an imaginary line across a ploughed field! It often takes several outings to devise the best possible off-road route that starts right from your front door. Expect the riding conditions to change radically from the height of summer to the depths of winter.

EXITS FROM LONDON

The best cycling 'escape routes' from London are along the watercourses of the River Thames and the canals. The Thames can be followed from Putney Bridge southwest to Weybridge (see Ride 5); from Weybridge it is possible to link via the Wey Navigation (see Ride 4) to the Basingstoke Canal which finishes near Odiham in deepest Hampshire (see Rides 1, 2 and 3). To the east, the Thames can be followed from Greenwich to Erith (see Ride 30); the Grand Union Canal starts near

Paddington and runs west to Hayes then north through Uxbridge to Rickmansworth and Watford. To the northeast, the Lee Valley offers an exit to Waltham Abbey, Ware and Hertford. The Grand Union Canal and the Lee & Stort Navigation are covered in another book in the series, *Cycling Traffic Free: Home Counties*.

SUSTRANS AND THE NATIONAL CYCLE NETWORK

The National Cycle Network is a linked series of traffic-free paths and traffic-calmed roads being developed right across the United Kingdom, linking town centres and the countryside. Visit Sustrans' website www.sustrans.org.uk for more details. In the region covered by this book there are three main National Cycle Network long distance routes covered by maps (see the Sustrans website):

1. **London to Oxford** (the Thames Valley Cycle Route). The first part of the route is covered by the sister publication, *Cycling Traffic Free: Home Counties.* Close to London the route largely follows the Thames riverside path from Putney Bridge to Weybridge (Ride 5).

2. **London to Eastbourne and Hastings** (the Downs & Weald Cycle Route). The route starts at Greenwich in London and goes south via what is known as the Waterlink Way running down through Deptford, Catford and Lewisham towards Croydon and Redhill. After crossing the High Weald to East Grinstead and using the Worth Way (Ride 18) and the Forest Way (Ride 19), the route soon joins the popular Cuckoo Trail (Ride 23) from Heathfield down to Polegate.

3. **London to Dover and Hastings** (the Garden of England Cycle Route). Running east of Greenwich and the Thames Barrier (Ride 30) National Cycle Network Route 1 continues along the Thames estuary then heads inland through Kent on to Canterbury (Ride 29). It rejoins the coast, picking up Ride 28 south of Deal, Ride 26 on the cliffs between Dover and Folkestone and Ride 25 along the promenade from Folkestone to Hythe.

THE COUNTRY CODE

- Enjoy the countryside and respect its life and work
- Guard against all risk of fire
- Fasten all gates
- Keep your dogs under close control
- Keep to rights of way across farmland
- Use gates and stiles to cross fences, hedges and walls
- Leave livestock, crops and machinery alone
- Take your litter home
- Help to keep all water clean
- Protect wildlife, plants and trees
- Take special care on country roads
- Make no unnecessary noise

Cycling Traffic-Free:
South East
The Main Routes

ROUTE 1
Basingstoke Canal from Fleet to the Greywell Tunnel (West of Odiham)

Distance: 10 miles one way, 20 miles return.
Map: Ordnance Survey Landranger map 186. GEOprojects produce a good map of the canal. Go to www.geoprojects.net/basingstoke.htm
Website: www.basingstoke-canal.co.uk
Hills: None.
Surface: Good stone-based track with occasional short rougher section.
Roads and road crossings: Several, although none are difficult.
Refreshments: Fox & Hounds pub, just west of Fleet; George & Lobster pub, Crookham Village; Barley Mow pub, Winchfield Hurst; Water Witch, Odiham; Jolly Miller pub, Swan pub, North Wanborough.

Running through Hampshire and Surrey, the canal originally linked Basingstoke to the junction with the River Wey Navigation near Weybridge. It has 29 locks, all but one in Surrey. The Basingstoke Canal is held by many to be Britain's most beautiful waterway. From the rolling hills of North Hampshire to the dramatic flights of locks in Surrey, the tree-lined canal offers a variety of delights, from 200 year old bridges and locks to traditionally painted narrow boats. This is the first of three sections of the canal which is described in the book, from Fleet to the tunnel at Greywell, passing the extraordinary ruins of Odiham Castle close to Greywell. The ride can be started at either end (or indeed in the middle – see 'Parking', below).

BACKGROUND AND PLACES OF INTEREST
Greywell Tunnel
Built in the late 18th century, the tunnel lasted for almost 150 years before collapsing in 1932. It now has huge ecological importance as a haven for bats. The blockage has created a cave-like environment with a constant temperature and high humidity. During the winter months it supports the second largest hibernating population of Natterer's bat in Europe.

War defences on the canal
Between Church Crookham and Dogmersfield the canal is dotted with pill boxes, tank traps and various wartime defences. These were built as part of a defence line running from Margate to Bristol. The Basingstoke Canal formed a useful lowland link in a chain which for the most part used steep natural slopes to slow the progress of the expected invasion.

Starting Points & Parking:

1. Fleet – small car park at the traffic lights at the junction of the B3013 with the A323 just south of the centre of Fleet (Grid reference SU 809537). This is at the junction of Reading Road South, Aldershot Road and Connaught Road. The car park is not easily spotted and has an open red and white metal barrier at the entrance. If this car park is full,

park along Connaught Road, opposite. Take care crossing back to the canal towpath.

2. Greywell Tunnel (Grid reference SU 719513), to the west of Odiham. This is the westernmost limit of the towpath. The nearest car park is at the northeast edge of Odiham, near the Water Witch pub (Grid reference SU 747517).

There are also car parks by the canal:

(a) southeast of Winchfield Hurst (near the Barley Mow pub)

(b) south of Crookham Village (near the George & Lobster pub)

ROUTE INSTRUCTIONS

From the small car park by the canal in the centre of Fleet follow the towpath southwest, keeping the water to your left. No instructions are needed as it is very straightforward to follow the canal. After about 9 miles and shortly after passing the extraordinary ruins of Odiham Castle (on your right) the towpath ends at the portal to Greywell Tunnel.

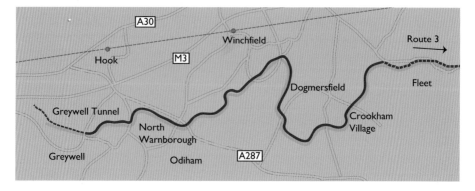

ROUTE 2
Basingstoke Canal from the Mytchett Canal Visitor Centre (Farnborough) to Fleet

Distance: 9 miles one way, 18 miles return.

Map: Ordnance Survey Landranger map 186. GEOprojects produce a good map of the canal. Go to www.geoprojects.net/basingstoke.htm

Website: www.basingstoke-canal.co.uk

Hills: None.

Surface: Mixed quality surfaces from fine gravel path to some narrower, stonier sections.

Roads and road crossings: No difficult road crossings.

Refreshments: Canal Visitor Centre Tea Room in Mytchett. Lots of choice in Fleet.

This is the middle section of the Basingstoke Canal and despite its proximity to the built-up areas along the Blackwater Valley it has a very green, woodland feel. It starts at the fascinating Visitor Centre at Mytchett (which also has a tearoom for when you get back after your ride) and heads south past Mytchett Lake and Greatbottom Flash. Pass high above the A331 dual carriageway running up the Blackwater Valley and continue across gorse- and heather-covered heathland to Fleet. You may wish to continue further west (see Ride 1) or indeed from the Visitor Centre you could just as easily head north then east towards Weybridge (Ride 3).

BACKGROUND AND PLACES OF INTEREST
History of the Basingstoke Canal
Originally completed in 1794, the canal was never a great commercial success for its owners. However it brought significant improvements for local people, industry and agriculture. As an example, the price of coal in Alton dropped by 50% after the canal opened. There were some boom periods for the owners, particularly during the construction of the army camp at Aldershot in the 1860s. The collapse of the Greywell Tunnel in 1934 effectively closed the link to Basingstoke. By the 1960s, the canal had fallen into dereliction but over a 17-year period (1974-1991) it was restored by volunteers and council staff.

Starting Points & Parking:
1. Canal Centre, Mytchett Place Road, Mytchett, southeast of the M3 Junction 4 (Grid reference SU 893551).

2. Fleet – small car park at the traffic lights at the junction of the B3013 with the A323 just south of the centre of Fleet (Grid reference SU 809537). This is at the junction of Reading Road South, Aldershot Road and Connaught Road. The car park is not easily spotted and has an open red and white metal barrier at the entrance. If this car park is full, park along Connaught Road, opposite. Take care crossing back to the canal towpath.

ROUTE INSTRUCTIONS:

1. From the Mytchett Canal Visitor Centre cross the bridge over the canal and turn left, keeping the water to your left. Soon go past Mytchett Lake and Greatbottom Flash.

2. Cross the viaduct over the A331 and the Blackwater River. The quality of the towpath deteriorates, then improves.

3. Pass through a landscape of heathland and gorse and beneath two big black metal 'meccano' style bridges.

4. The suggested turnaround point is the centre of Fleet where there is a choice of pubs and cafes, but if you wish to carry on, the canal continues for a further 10 miles to the tunnel at Greywell. (Join Ride 1, page 18).

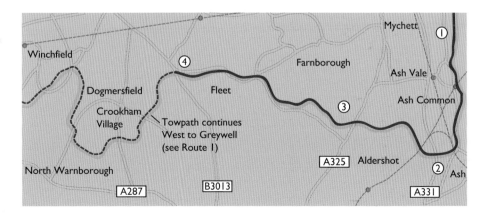

ROUTE 3

Basingstoke Canal: Mytchett Canal Visitor Centre to Byfleet and the Junction with the Wey Navigation

Distance: 13 miles one way, 26 miles return.

Map: Ordnance Survey Landranger maps 186 and 187. GEOprojects produce a good map of the canal. Go to www.geoprojects.net/basingstoke.htm

Website: www.basingstoke-canal.co.uk

Hills: None

Surface: Variable surface from the excellent fine gravel section through Woking to some rougher stretches elsewhere.

Roads and road crossings: Several road crossings, some of which may be busy.

Refreshments: Tearoom at Canal Visitor Centre at Mytchett.
Lots of cafes and pubs just off the route through Woking.

The third and final ride on the Basingstoke Canal, from the Visitor Centre at Mytchett to the canal's junction with the Wey Navigation near to Byfleet. The ride is predominantly on a wide stone and gravel track through beautiful broadleaf woodland, especially noticeable through the remarkable flight of locks at Deepcut where there are 14 locks in less than two miles. The best quality towpath on the whole of the canal runs through Woking: wide and smooth with the vegetation cut well back away from the path – a real delight to ride. The end of the canal at its junction with the Wey Navigation is right underneath the M25 and as this is not an especially exciting place you may prefer to continue north up towards Weybridge or south towards Pyrford for refreshments.

Starting Points & Parking:

1. Canal Centre, Mytchett Place Road, Mytchett, off the B3411 between Frimley and Ash, southeast of M3 Junction 4 (Grid reference SU 893551).

2. There are several Pay & Display car parks in Woking and West Byfleet close to the canal.

ROUTE INSTRUCTIONS:

1. From the Mytchett Canal Visitor Centre, cross the canal and turn right, keeping the canal to your right.

2. After ¾ mile at the B3012 (opposite the King's Head pub) turn right, then left to rejoin the canal towpath. The railway line passes under the canal.

3. There may be a 1-mile diversion away from the canal east of the B3015 - follow signs on a track parallel with and to the north of the canal.

4. Rejoin the canal and follow through Brookwood, close to the railway line. The towpath quality improves dramatically at the western edge of Woking.

5. In central Woking you will need to cross Chobham Road using the traffic lights to regain the towpath on the other side.

6. The suggested end point is at the junction with the Wey Navigation beneath the M25. However this is not a very exciting place and you may prefer to follow the Wey Navigation north to Weybridge for 2 miles to find refreshments or south for 2 miles to the pub at Pyrford Lock (see Route 4 on page 27).

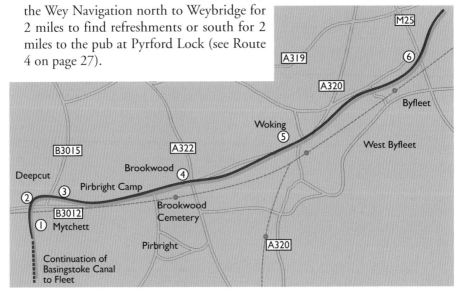

Distance: 5 miles one way, 10 miles return.

Map: Ordnance Survey Landranger maps 176 & 187. The Surrey Cycle Guides provide more detail: go to www.surreycc.gov.uk and put 'Surrey Cycle Guide' into the 'Search' box to find out how to order copies. The Wey Navigation is also covered by the Basingstoke Canal GEOproject map – go to www.geoprojects.net/basingstoke.htm

Hills: There are no hills.

Surface: Stone- and gravel-based towpath, with some rougher sections near the start.

Roads and road crossings: There is a very short section on road at the start of the ride, then several quiet roads to be crossed during the middle part of the ride.

Refreshments: Minnow pub, Old Crown Inn at the start. Anchor pub, Pyrford Lock.

There are several traffic-free options for escaping from southwest London along the waterways. The Thames Towpath runs from Putney Bridge to Weybridge and the Basingstoke Canal starts south of Weybridge and runs southwest through Woking to Odiham in Hampshire. Connecting the two and taking a more southerly course, the Wey Navigation starts in Weybridge and heads through Byfleet towards Guildford and Godalming. The middle section of the canal towpath (from Pyrford to Guildford) is fairly rough but the 5-mile stretch described below is in reasonable condition and offers a chance to enjoy a ride along a green corridor through this built-up area ending at a waterside pub at Pyrford Lock.

BACKGROUND AND PLACES OF INTEREST

The Wey Navigations

Opened in 1653, this waterway is one of the oldest in the country. It runs for 20 miles from Godalming to Weybridge and is the southernmost link in Britain's 2000-mile canal network. Timber, coal, corn, flour and even gunpowder were regularly moved up and down the waterway. Later, in 1796, the Basingstoke Canal was dug and connected to the Wey and in 1816 the Wey and Arun Junction Canal was opened, connecting with the Wey at Stonebridge.

Starting Points & Parking:

1. Weybridge – the riverside car park just north of Weybridge on the sharp bend on Thames Street/Walton Lane (GR TQ 076658). If this is full you can also park at the much larger car park by Walton Bridge (Grid Reference TQ 094663) then follow the Thames towpath westwards to this point.

2. Pyrford Lock, west of the A3/M25 junction (Grid reference TQ 054593).

ROUTE INSTRUCTIONS:

1. Exit the riverside car park on Walton Lane/Thames Street and bear right towards the Minnow pub. Immediately before the Old Crown pub turn right down Church Walk (by the Public Conveniences). Dismount and walk for 50 yards.

2. At the end of the path turn right, cross the ornate metal bridge then at the T-junction turn left signposted 'Flockton House' and shortly turn right onto a wide gravel path alongside green railings. Dismount to cross a humpback metal bridge and turn left on the towpath.

3. At times narrow and rooty. After ¾ mile, at a grey-brick bridge at the T-junction with Addlestone Road, turn right, signposted 'Addlestone/Chertsey Bike Route'. You may prefer to ride on the road parallel to the canal as a more comfortable option for ¼ mile as far as the humpback bridge on your left where the towpath changes sides.

4. You will occasionally need to cross roads and the towpath changes sides. Pass beneath the M25* following signs for Guildford and Godalming. It is suggested you continue for 2 miles beyond the canal junction as far as the Anchor pub at Pyrford Marina then return to Weybridge. About 1 mile beyond Pyrford Marina the towpath becomes much rougher.

* *At the point where you pass under the M25 you have the option of turning right off the Wey Navigation and following the Basingstoke Canal for many miles through Woking, Aldershot and Fleet to Odiham. See Rides 1, 2 and 3.*

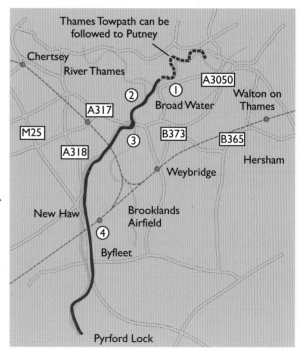

ROUTE 5
Thames Towpath from Weybridge to Putney Bridge

Distance: Up to 22 miles one way, 44 miles return. Clearly, as this is a linear ride, it can be broken down into several shorter sections and ridden towards or away from central London. The train can also be used for one leg of the trip. Good halfway points are Kingston, Richmond or the car park by the river to the north of Ham House (Grid reference TQ 170732).

Map: Ordnance Survey Landranger map 176. A street map of London would be just as helpful or the Transport for London Cycle Guides: see www.tfl.gov.uk/cycling

Hills: None.

Surface: Good stone-based tracks, tarmac. One slightly rougher section between Ham and Richmond and another near to Chiswick Bridge.

Roads and road crossings: Several short sections of minor residential roads. The towpath changes sides twice:, at Hampton Court Bridge then at Kingston Bridge where there are cycle lanes to take you through the centre of Kingston to regain the riverside path. There is ⅓ mile east of Barnes a railway bridge where there is no towpath and you are advised to walk along the pavement.

Refreshments: There are refreshment opportunities all along the route, too numerous to mention. The greatest choice right by the riverside is in Richmond.

The Thames towpath represents the best cycling escape from London, offering an almost unbroken traffic-free option from Putney Bridge right down to Weybridge. For the very adventurous it would be possible to link the Thames towpath via the Wey Navigation (Ride 4) to the Basingstoke Canal (Rides 1, 2 and 3) to create a 55-mile traffic free ride to Greywell in Hampshire, just east of Basingstoke. For those with more modest aims, the ride can be broken down into many shorter sections. There are many highlights such as the ornate bridges spanning the Thames, the fine buildings of Richmond and the stunning facade of Hampton Court, but more than anything, the defining characteristic of such a ride is the wonderful sense of space that it offers.

NB Much of this ride will be very popular with pedestrians on fine summer weekends so take your time and give people plenty of warning. Better still, choose a quiet time mid-week, early morning or evening.

Starting Point & Parking:
The riverside car park on the sharp bend on Thames Street/Walton Lane to the north of Weybridge (GR TQ 076658). If this is full you can also park at the much larger car park by Walton Bridge in Walton on Thames and join the river a little further downstream (Grid reference TQ 094664).

ROUTE INSTRUCTIONS:
1. Follow the Thames towpath towards central London with the river to your left. About 2 miles after Walton Bridge you will need to dismount through Sunbury Lock.

2. After a further 3 miles, and shortly after Molesey Lock, join the pavement and cross Hampton Court Bridge over the Thames following signs for National Cycle Network Route 4 and Hampton Court. Go past the stunning buildings of Hampton Court and the grounds of Hampton Court Park.

3. Follow close to the river for 3 miles. At Kingston Bridge, stay on this (south) side of the bridge and carefully follow the green painted cycle lanes and signs

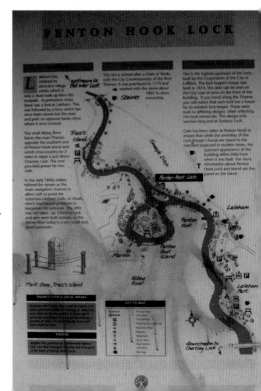

for 'National Cycle Network Route 4', 'Thames Cycle Route' and 'Ham, Twickenham, Richmond' to pass around John Lewis, keeping the store on your left. Cross several roads via toucan crossings. Rejoin the river at the end of Downhall Road. Pass under an arch of mature plane trees.

4. About 2 miles after Kingston Bridge, as National Cycle Network Route 4 turns right towards Ham and Richmond Park, stay close to the river. The surface quality becomes a bit rougher. The surface turns to tarmac through Richmond then back to gravel.

5. Pass under Kew Bridge. Shortly after the Ship pub near Chiswick Bridge there is a short, narrow section which may be covered in exceptionally high tides, in which case you will need to negotiate a way around this point via Mortlake High Street to return to the towpath further along.

6. There is a third of a mile beyond Barnes railway bridge where there is no towpath and it is recommended you dismount and push your bikes on the pavement alongside Lonsdale Road to rejoin the towpath.

7. Pass under the ornate structure of Hammersmith Bridge. After 1¼ miles the towpath joins a residential road (Embankment) to finish at Putney Bridge.

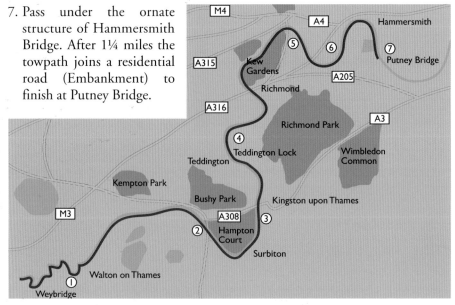

ROUTE 6

The Tamsin Trail around Richmond Park in south west London

Distance: 8-mile circuit.

Map: Ordnance Survey Landranger map 176. Better is the map which you can buy from the Information Centre at Pembroke Lodge or the Transport for London Cycle Guides: see www.tfl.gov.uk/cycling

Website: www.royalparks.org.uk/parks/richmond_park

Hills: The two highest points in Richmond Park are near Pembroke Lodge on the west side of the park and on Broomfield Hill on the southeast edge. There are climbs up to these and descents from them whether you choose to go clockwise or anti-clockwise.

Surface: Good stone-based tracks, tarmac.

Roads and road crossings: At each vehicle entrance to the gate there are roads to cross and care should be taken, especially if you are with young children.

Refreshments: There are two cafes on the Tamsin Trail, at Pembroke Lodge and at Roehampton Gate near the Bike Hire.

Cycle Hire: At Roehampton Gate (April to September). 07050 209 249.

This is a fantastic traffic-free circuit of London's largest Royal Park offering fine views out over the city, a chance to get close to the deer, cafe stops for tired legs and a chance to extend the ride by linking to the Thames towpath (see Ride 5 on page 30). With its 2500 acres of hills, woods, lakes and famous herds of deer, Richmond Park is only 10 miles from the centre of London, but offers a real escape from the noise and fumes of the city streets. It is the largest and wildest of the Royal Parks. For hundreds of years it was used as a royal hunting ground; in 1637 King Charles I built an 8-mile brick wall around the park to stop his 2000 deer from straying.

Starting Point & Parking:

As this is a circular route it can be joined at any one of the several gates into the park. Clockwise these are:

Sheen Gate (vehicles, parking).

Roehampton Gate (vehicles, parking, cafe, bike hire).

Robin Hood Gate (pedestrian access only).

Kingston Gate (vehicles, parking).

Ham Gate (vehicles, parking and cafe at Pembroke Lodge).

Petersham Gate (pedestrian access only).

Richmond Gate (vehicles, parking and cafe at Pembroke Lodge).

Bishop's Gate, Cambrian Gate, Bog Gate (pedestrian access only).

ROUTE INSTRUCTIONS:

No instructions are given, as this is a well-signposted circular route around the perimeter of the park, which can be ridden either clockwise or anti-clockwise. Take care when crossing the five roads which come into the park.

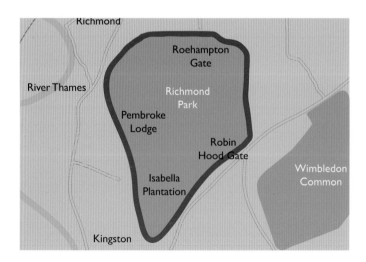

Distance: Two circuits, each of 3 miles.

Map/leaflet: Ordnance Survey Landranger map 187. The Surrey Cycle Guides provide more detail: go to www.surreycc.gov.uk and put 'Surrey Cycle Guide' into the 'Search' box to find out how to order copies.

Website: www.sustainable-epsom.fsnet.co.uk > Transport > Cycling > Networks & Maps

Hills: There are a few gentle hills.

Surface: Good quality gravel tracks.

Roads and road crossings: Take care crossing the B280 which runs east-west between the two circuits.

Refreshments: None on the route, the closest are in Epsom itself.

Starting Point & Parking:
From the centre of Epsom follow the B280 west towards the A243. Go straight ahead at two closely spaced roundabouts then after ½ mile keep an eye out for the entrance to a woodland car park on your left (Grid reference TQ 183611). There is also a car park on Horton Lane to the north of the second roundabout (Grid reference TQ 190616).

ROUTE INSTRUCTIONS:
HORTON PARK CIRCUIT

1. Exit the car park back towards the B280, then turn sharp right by the wooden barrier to go past an information board. At the lake turn left uphill. At the top of the hill by a wooden barrier and a post with yellow and blue arrows bear left, signposted 'Chessington Countryside Walk'.

2. At a white wooden fence cross the B280 with care onto the track opposite 'Bridleway Horton Lane'. Join tarmac, go past West Park Hospital and bear left onto the cycle path 'Tolworth, Kingston'. Follow an 'Access to Horton Country Park' sign and shortly bear right off tarmac onto a gravel track to the right of a wooden fence.

3. At a major track crossroads, go straight ahead 'Horseride, Chessington Countryside Walk' (the track to the left is the return route). Ignore a left turn. Shortly at a fork of tracks with low wooden posts to the right, bear right.

4. Gentle descent. At the T-junction by large concrete slabs turn right. Go past a pond and between golf greens. At the crossroads of tracks at the top of a short rise turn left. Bear right at a series of forks.

5. At the track T-junction with a narrow grass track ahead turn left. At the crossroads of tracks by a red tile-hung house turn right to join the outward route.

EPSOM COMMON CIRCUIT

A. Start as per Horton Park circuit, but instead of crossing the B280, continue on the track parallel with the road on its south side.

B. At the T-junction of tracks by two wooden barriers turn right, then left. Stay on the broad, stone-based track as it meanders through woodland.

C. At the junction of tracks by a 'Winter horse ride' sign and the back of a large green ('Epsom Common') signboard, bear right 'Ashtead Common'.

D. At a fork of tracks by a wooden signpost with blue and yellow arrows bear right 'Bike Route'. At the T-junction with a bench ahead turn right.

E. After ½ mile at a crossroads of tracks turn right 'Christchurch Road ⅓ mile'. At the bottom of the descent turn left opposite the pond to return to the start.

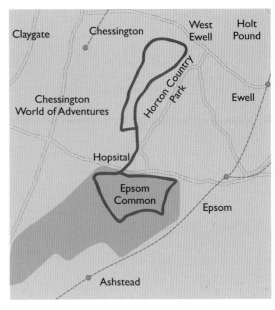

ROUTE 8
Alice Holt Forest, southwest of Farnham in Surrey

Distance: A 3-mile circuit.

Map/leaflet: Ordnance Survey Landranger map 186 or there is a leaflet, *Explore Alice Holt Forest*, available from the Visitor Centre.

Website: www.forestry.gov.uk/aliceholt

Hills: There are several gentle hills.

Surface: Good quality gravel tracks all the way round.

Roads and road crossings: There are no road crossings.

Refreshments: The shop/Visitor Centre sells drinks and ice creams.

Cycle Hire: Quench Cycles (01580 879694) or go to their website: www.quenchuk.co.uk

A well-waymarked route around the gently undulating mixed broadleaf and conifer woodlands in Alice Holt Woodland Park to the southwest of Farnham. There is a good cycle hire centre offering a variety of bikes and trailers. There are plenty of other activities in the forest including the Playwood Playground, the Three Dimensional Wooden Maze, the Timberline Assault Course, the Habitat Adventure Trail, and of course, Go Ape.

BACKGROUND AND PLACES OF INTEREST

History of the forest

Important potteries were developed in Alice Holt in Roman times as a result of the proximity of local resources: local clay for the pots, heathland turf for the kilns and forest timber for the fuel. You can see a reconstructed pottery kiln in Goose Green Enclosure. Many hundreds of years later, the forest was owned by Aelfsige, Bishop of Winchester, and it is thought to be named after him. The Old English name of Aelfsige's Holt became Alice Holt.

From the Middle Ages onwards, timber was the woodland's most prized resource, the trees being used to build ships for Britain's navy. Hundreds of mature oaks were needed to build a single ship and the forest was periodically stripped of its large trees to supply the naval

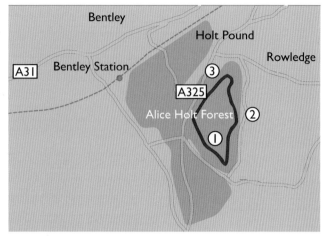

shipyards dotted along the south coast. Alice Holt oak has been used to build the replica of Shakespeare's Globe Theatre in London.

Starting Point & Parking:
Alice Holt Visitor Centre is just off the A325 Farnham–Petersfield road, 4 miles southwest of Farnham (Grid reference SU 812416).

ROUTE INSTRUCTIONS:
1. From the car park go past the cafe and a second wooden building. You will see a tall square wooden post indicating the start of the Family Cycle Trail.

2. Follow the numbered posts. The route starts with a long gentle downhill (Posts 1-13) then climbs, with the steepest section from Posts 18-20.

3. Keep following the numbered posts, with the occasional wide ranging view and a visit to Lodge Pond, to return to the start.

Distance: There are two waymarked trails:

1. The purple-topped posts waymark a 3.7-mile circuit, with hills, but suitable for all.
2. The orange-topped posts waymark a 3.1-mile advanced mountain bike trail for experienced riders with good technical skills.

There are also routes waymarked with a blue arrow/white bicycle. These go out of the park into the surrounding countryside and occasionally use roads. For further details ask in the Visitor Centre for the Off-road Cycle Trail Pack.

Map/leaflet: Ordnance Survey Landranger map 197. Much better is the excellent A2 full colour 'Queen Elizabeth Country Park Trails Guide' available from the Visitor Centre.

Hills: There is one major hill with over 400 ft of climbing, parts of which you may well choose to walk. In general terms the purple (easier) route climbs steadily for the first half of the route and descends for the second half.

Surface: Good quality gravel tracks.

Roads and road crossings: No road crossings.

Refreshments: Cafe at the Visitor Centre.

Queen Elizabeth Country Park is certainly not flat but there is an excellent waymarked traffic-free circuit through stunning beech woodland and plenty of other attractions in the park and at the Visitor Centre. For the more adventurous there is a technically challenging mountain bike circuit. There are also trails leading out of the park onto the network of bridleways and lanes that criss-cross the South Downs, the great chalk ridge stretching from Winchester to Eastbourne.

NB Children should be supervised closely on the downhill sections as it is possible to pick up a lot of speed quite quickly!

BACKGROUND AND PLACES OF INTEREST
Queen Elizabeth Country Park
The park is part of the landscape of the South Downs and is in an Area of Outstanding Natural Beauty. It covers 1400 acres and is dominated by the three hills of Butser, War Down and Holt Down, which provide a contrast between the dramatic downland and beautiful woodland. With 38 species of butterfly and 12 species of wild orchid, it is a naturalist's paradise, a large area of which is designated as a Site of Special Scientific Interest. The many Roman and Iron Age sites in the park are also preserved as Scheduled Ancient Monuments.

Starting Point & Parking: Queen Elizabeth Country Park is well signposted off the A3 to the southwest of Petersfield (on the way to Portsmouth). There is a Pay & Display car park by the Visitor Centre and further car parks beyond this if the first car park is full (Grid reference SU 719185).

ROUTE INSTRUCTIONS:

The routes are well signposted. The trails start from the corner of the car park to the left of the Visitor Centre by a large colourful carved wooden signpost (or alternatively go through the first car park and onto the Gravel Hill car park).

1. From the carved signpost take the upper path (cycle link route) indicated by the orange/purple signpost (*NOT* the lower path closer to the Visitor Centre). After ¼ mile cross the road via wooden barriers into the car park opposite to find the start of the easy trail (by a purple bike sign with a white border).

2. Briefly join the road, then on a sharp left-hand hairpin bend bear right onto a wide gravel track (purple bike sign). Long steady climb. Go past a wooden 'stable' and turn left off the main stone track onto a narrower track (purple bike sign).

3. The climb gets ever steeper – can you make it before turning sharp right by red-topped posts where the path temporarily levels off? At the T-junction with a broad track turn left to climb to the highpoint.

4. Long gentle descent. Easy to miss: after several 'Straight on' purple bike signs keep an eye out for a left turn. Complete the loop by the 'stable' and turn right to rejoin the outward route. At the road (hairpin bend) bear left, then left again. At the car park go straight ahead onto the 'link' route to return to the Visitor Centre.

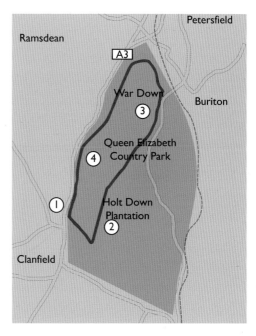

ROUTE 10
Centurion Way from West Dean to Chichester

Distance: 5 miles one way, 10 miles return.

Map/leaflet: Ordnance Survey Landranger map 197. A leaflet about the Centurion Way can be downloaded from: www.westsussex.gov.uk and search 'Centurion Way leaflet'

Hills: There is a short hill between the cycle path alongside the A286 and the railway path, about one mile south of West Dean.

Surface: Good quality gravel track. One short rough section connecting the A286 cycle path to the railway path.

Roads and road crossings: None on the route. You will need to use roads if you are starting from/visiting the centre of Chichester.

Refreshments: Selsey Arms pub in West Dean. Lots of choice in Chichester.

This railway path and dedicated cycle path runs between West Dean and Chichester, passing some extraordinary metal sculptures of Roman centurions and 'surveyors'. The route passes through woodland and arable land with a profusion of wildflowers along the verges. The name Centurion Way was suggested by a local schoolboy and is based on the fact that the path crosses the course of a Roman Road. At its southern end the path can easily be linked to the Chichester Canal towpath or to the Salterns Way (see Ride 11).

BACKGROUND AND PLACES OF INTEREST
History of the railway
The Chichester to Midhurst Railway was opened in 1881 to improve access to London. The line included three tunnels and eight stations, the most notable of the latter being Singleton, due to its proximity to Goodwood Racecourse. The railway's decline started with the withdrawal of passenger services in 1935 and the line north of Lavant was closed completely in 1957. The section between Lavant and Chichester was subsequently used for freight until 1991. In 1994 the County Council purchased the railway line and with investment and help from English Partnerships, Chichester District Council and Tarmac Quarry Products the old railway line was converted to recreational use.

Starting Points & Parking:
1. From Midhurst/the north – turn left off the A286 in West Dean onto the minor road by the Selsey Arms pub towards West Dean Stores. At the bottom turn right and park along here (Grid reference SU 858122).

2. Chichester – the southern end of the path is on the west side of Chichester near to Bishop Luffa School (Grid reference SU 848047). Follow West Street/Westgate from the centre of Chichester, straight over a roundabout and park on the road before the railings/level crossing. To join the trail take the tarmac path by the school then shortly turn left onto the Centurion Way.

ROUTE INSTRUCTIONS:
1. Follow the minor road in West Dean southwards to join the A286 and turn left along the dedicated cycle path alongside the main road.

2. After 1 mile, at the end of the A286 cycle path, with a red letter box set in a brick wall ahead, turn left downhill on a rough track, soon joining the railway path running along the valley.

3. At the houses in Mid Lavant aim for the far right-hand corner of the 'green' then

turn left. Continue in the same direction, ignoring turns to the left. Pass between concrete bollards and as the road swings right bear left onto Churchmead Close, signposted 'Chichester'. Take the next left on Warbleheath Close, signposted 'Chichester' to rejoin the railway path.

4. Gentle descent over almost 3 miles to Chichester, passing the extraordinary metal sculptures of surveyors. At the end of the path at Bishop Luffa School:

(a) retrace your steps back to West Dean

(b) turn left and continue in the same direction along West Gate and West Street to visit the cathedral and the centre of Chichester (there is some traffic on these roads)

(c) turn left, then after ½ mile turn right onto Mount Lane and follow signs for 'Railway station, Hunston' to access the Chichester Canal, the towpath of which can be followed for about 2 miles, as far as the A286

(d) turn right, cross the level crossing and bear right to link up with the Salterns Way (Ride 11, page 50).

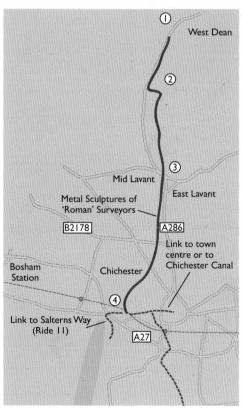

ROUTE 11

Salterns Way, South of Chichester

Distance: 11 miles one way, 22 miles return.

Map: Ordnance Survey Landranger map 197. A leaflet can be downloaded from www.conservancy.co.uk > Out & About > Cycling

Hills: None.

Surface: Good stone-based tracks, roads.

Roads and road crossings:

There are several road sections on this route and although they are mainly quiet, only the traffic-free sections of this route are appropriate for young children.

Refreshments: Lots of choice in Chichester. Pub just off the route in West Itchenor.

Lots of choice in West Wittering (this involves using the busy B2179).

The Salterns Way links the centre of Chichester, the marina and the coast at West Wittering using a mixture of quiet roads and specially-built cycle paths. The final section into West Wittering is only suitable for experienced cyclists but there are some excellent sections up to this point that are appropriate for casual cyclists (although not young children, as this route is not predominantly traffic-free).

BACKGROUND AND PLACES OF INTEREST
Chichester Canal
The waterway is part of the Portsmouth & Arundel Canal which linked with other rivers and navigations to form an inland waterway route between London and Portsmouth. Designed by John Rennie (1761-1821), the Portsmouth & Arundel Canal was opened in 1822 and remained in operation as a through route until 1855. The Chichester section between the harbour and the city was constructed as a ship canal permitting passage for vessels up to 85ft long and weighing as much as 100 tons.

Starting Points & Parking:
1. Chichester Cathedral, in the centre of Chichester (Grid reference SU 859047).

2. Chichester Marina, off the A286 about 3 miles south of Chichester (Grid reference SU 835011).

ROUTE INSTRUCTIONS:

1. With your back to Chichester Cathedral turn left along West Street. At the large roundabout take the second exit signposted '7.5 ton weight limit' onto a road paved with red bricks.

2. At the mini-roundabout continue in same direction on Westgate Street, signposted 'South Coast Cycle Route'. Follow to the end of the road towards the metal fencing and go over the level crossing. At the T-junction bear right.

3. Pass through the subway under the A27 then at a crossroads of tracks turn left. Cross the busy A259 via the traffic island and turn left on the pavement cycle path.

4. Shortly turn first right onto Appledram Lane for ¼ mile. Use the pavement if preferred. Keep an eye out for a left turn onto a track just after the barn and farm on the left. Follow the field edge path.

5. At the end of the track turn left on the road. At the T-junction turn right signposted 'Dell Quay' then shortly turn left by a 'Quay Quarters' sign towards Apuldram Manor Farm 'Salterns Way'.

6. At the T-junction at the end of the woodland track, with the marina ahead, turn left. At the T-junction by a large information board turn right, signposted 'Salterns Way'. Pass to the left of Chichester Yacht Club and cross the canal.

7. Bear right at a fork of footpaths ('Salterns Way') then at the T-junction with Lock Lane turn left. At the T-junction at the end of Martins Lane turn right, signposted 'Salterns Way'.

8. Follow the road to the left past the church and continue in the same direction onto a no through road, 'Westlands, Greenacres'. Tarmac turns to a concrete farm track. About 200 yards before a large grey barn turn left, signposted 'Salterns Way'.

9. Meandering stone-based field edge path. At the T-junction with the road turn right (remember this point for the return). Busier road. Shortly after the flint church of St Nicholas, on a sharp right-hand bend, turn left, signposted 'Salterns Way' *. Pass to the left of the white posts for Itchenor Park House.

* *OR continue straight ahead for the pub in West Itchenor*

10. Stone-based field edge path. Follow 'Salterns Way' signs closely. At the T-junction with a concrete farm road turn left. Turn right off the concrete track onto a field edge path then shortly right at a T-junction. Stop at the B2179 (Rookwood Road) on the north side of West Wittering. Unless you are experienced cyclists or it is mid-week out of season, it is best to turn around here as this road gets very busy.

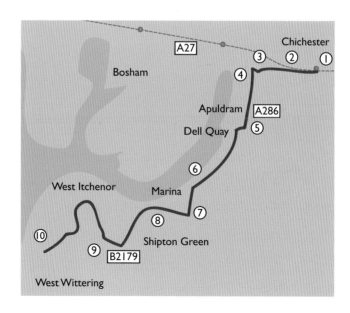

ROUTE 12
Wey Navigation from Guildford to Godalming

Distance: 4½ miles one way, 9 miles return.
Map: Ordnance Survey Landranger map 186. The Surrey Cycle Guides provide more detail: go to www.surreycc.gov.uk and put 'Surrey Cycle Guide' into the 'Search' box to find out how to order copies.
Website: www.weyriver.co.uk/theriver/wey_nav_1.htm or also try www.nationaltrust.org.uk and search for 'Wey Navigation'.
Hills: None.
Surface: Mixed quality. Some rough, some sandy, some smooth gravel
Roads and road crossings: Two road crossings, both of which may be busy.
Refreshments: Lots of choice in Guildford. Hector's Tearoom at Farncombe. Lots of choice in Godalming.

Two sections of the Wey Navigation are suitable for cycling - both are described in this guide (see also Ride 4). The canal was part of a series of waterways connecting London to Portsmouth via the River Arun and Chichester Harbour. The quality of the towpath is variable and mountain bikes are recommended. It is easy to link this ride to the Downs Link at a point close to where the railway crosses the canal to the west of Shalford. Look out for the extraordinary cliffs of yellow sand at the northern end of the trail.

BACKGROUND AND PLACES OF INTEREST

Catteshall Lock

Catteshall Lock was built in 1764 and is the last lock on the Godalming Navigation. This was a busy spot throughout the 18th and 19th century. Barges transported large quantities of government stores and ammunition to Godalming from where it was taken on to the naval arsenal at Portsmouth. The 1830s were the highpoint of the waterways when tonnage carried was at its highest. Competition from the railways began to take away trade from the waterways from the 1840s onwards.

Second World War 2 defences

Over 5,000 pill boxes were built in the early 1940s as part of the inland GHQ defence line. The Wey Navigation was the last of a number of defence lines protecting the capital and key industrial areas. This line extended from the West Coast near Bristol to the Kent Coast near Chatham. Pill-box positions took advantage of natural and man-made obstacles such as rivers, canals and embankments and housed machine-gun and anti-tank weapons. There are similar pill boxes on the Basingstoke Canal and the Kennet & Avon Canal.

Starting Points & Parking:

1. Guildford: Mill Mead car park, by the council offices, off the High Street between the A3100 Portsmouth Road and the A281 Shalford Road (Grid reference SU 995493).

2. Godalming: in the main car park by Waitrose in the centre of town (Grid reference SU 973440). Walk your bike across the bridge over the River Wey and turn right onto the towpath by the Godalming United Church.

ROUTE INSTRUCTIONS:

1. From the south end of Mill Mead in Guildford (by the council offices and the Britannia pub), cross the river into the park and follow the path alongside the Wey Navigation, keeping the water to your left, soon passing the Guildford Rowing Club.

2. The quality of the towpath varies. After about 1½ miles pass under a railway bridge.

If you wish to join the Downs Link ride, about 100 yards after the railway bridge keep an eye out for an old World War 2 pill box up to your right. This is the start of the Downs Link. The surface quality improves after about ½ mile.

3. Stay on the towpath and cross the busy A248 (take care) then after a further mile cross the next road by Farncombe Boat House and Hector's Tearoom.

4. The towpath ends near the Godalming United Church just north of the bridge over the river in Godalming.

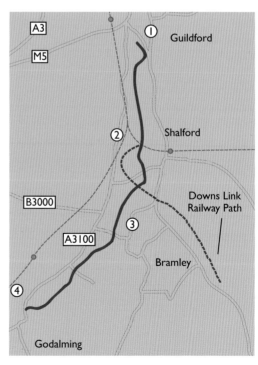

Distance: 6 miles one way, 12 miles return.

Map: Ordnance Survey Landranger map 186. A leaflet about the Downs Link can be downloaded from:www.westsussex.gov.uk and search 'Downs Link'

Hills: None.

Surface: Tarmac or good stone-based track.

Roads and road crossings: The A281 at the start is crossed via a traffic island.

Refreshments: Lots of choice in Cranleigh.

The Downs Link runs largely along the course of old disused railways from the North Downs Way on St Martha's Hill (to the east of Guildford) to the South Downs Way near to Shoreham. The easiest place to join the railway path close to Guildford is at the car park by the mast on the A281 to the south of Shalford. The trail starts with a tarmac surface and passes through delightful woodland on its way south to Cranleigh, full of bluebells in late spring. The trip between Bramley and Cranleigh offers a 12-mile round trip but as it is a linear ride it could easily be shortened or indeed extended beyond Cranleigh: the Downs Link continues for many miles towards the South Coast. There is also the option of going north from the car park to join the towpath of the Wey Navigation into Guildford or Godalming.

Starting Points & Parking:

1. Bramley/Shalford – the car park at the junction of the A281 with Trunley Heath Road, between Shalford and Bramley, south of Guildford (Grid reference SU 999462).

2. Cranleigh – the main car park just off the High Street by the clocktower (Grid reference TQ 050393).

ROUTE INSTRUCTIONS:

1. From the Trunley Heath Road car park, cross the busy A281 via the traffic island onto the Downs Link heading southeast. The path initially has a tarmac surface.

2. After 1 mile cross the road by the old Bramley station. The tarmac ends after a further mile and the trail is now a wide stone and gravel path.

3. Follow the path for a further 4 miles until arriving in Cranleigh – there is a large car park to your left*. At this point you can:

(a) visit Cranleigh for refreshments.

(b) turn around to return to the start point north of Bramley for a 12-mile round trip.

(c) continue further south on the Downs Link (see Ride 14, on page 60).

* *If you miss the car park you will come to a road crossing with the back of the Marks & Spencer's building in sight. This road can be busy so it is better to retrace your steps to the car park if you wish to go into Cranleigh.*

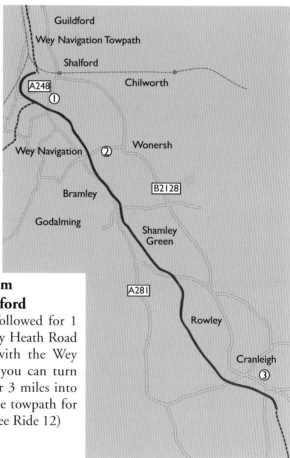

Extension northwest from the A281 towards Guildford

The railway path can be followed for 1 mile north from the Trunley Heath Road car park to its junction with the Wey Navigation. At this point you can turn right along the towpath for 3 miles into Godalming or left along the towpath for 1½ miles into Guildford. (see Ride 12)

ROUTE 14
The Downs Link from Cranleigh to Slinfold

Distance: 7 miles from Cranleigh to Slinfold, 14 miles return.

Map: Ordnance Survey Landranger map 187. A leaflet about the Downs Link can be downloaded from: www.westsussex.gov.uk and search 'Downs Link'

Hills: One short steep climb beyond Baynards.

Surface: Stone-based tracks, with some muddy puddles after rain and through the winter.

Roads and road crossings: One busy road to cross (A281) about halfway between Cranleigh and Slinfold. The last ½ mile into Slinfold is on a quiet lane.

Refreshments: Lots of choice in Cranleigh. Robert Fortune's Tea Hut (open June, July August and Bank Holidays) between Cranleigh and Baynards (01483 278582 or 07971 595181). Red Lyon pub, Slinfold.

This is the second section of the Downs Link described in the book. If you are fit you could link them all together for a tough day-long challenge. In its entirety, the 32-mile route links the North Downs Way and South Downs Way and is open to cyclists, walkers and horse riders. The ride starts with a long section through overarching broadleaf woodland which is carpeted with bluebells in spring. It can also get muddy after wet weather. In order to avoid a blocked tunnel just south of Baynards the trail needs to climb steeply up over the hill – an unexpected climb on what is otherwise a flat railway path. After the one busy road crossing (A281) you can descend off the path to see the famous double bridge which gives the Downs Link its logo. Slinfold is suggested as a turnaround point as there is a pub there.

BACKGROUND AND PLACES OF INTEREST
The old railway
The original railway was built in two stages: the first in 1861 by the London, Brighton & South Coast Railway from the coast to Christ's Hospital and the second in 1865 by the Horsham & Guildford Direct Railway Company from Christ's Hospital to Guildford. Neither line achieved the glory hoped for by the builders and after a century of use both railways fell to the Beeching Axe in 1966. Across Great Britain 2,300 railway stations and 4,000 miles of line closed.

The two-tiered bridge near Rudgwick
This unusual bridge over the Arun gives the Downs Link its logo. The higher bridge was built because the railway inspector was not happy with the steep gradient (1:80) to Rudgwick Station using the lower bridge. The embankments were raised and the iron girder bridge was built on top of the brick arch, creating a more gentle gradient of 1:130. (You will need to descend from the trail into the woods to see it properly).

Starting Point & Parking:
The main car park in Cranleigh (southeast of Guildford). The car park entrance is near to the ornate clock in Stocklund Square and to the NatWest Bank in the High Street. Park in the furthest corner to be near the start of the track (Grid Reference TQ 050393).

ROUTE INSTRUCTIONS:

1. Exit the corner of the Cranleigh car park and turn left. After 300 yards cross the road towards Marks & Spencer's (take care) then shortly turn right by low wooden posts, signposted 'Downs Link'. Follow the track/lane between playing fields. Continue for 3½ miles to the old station at Baynards.

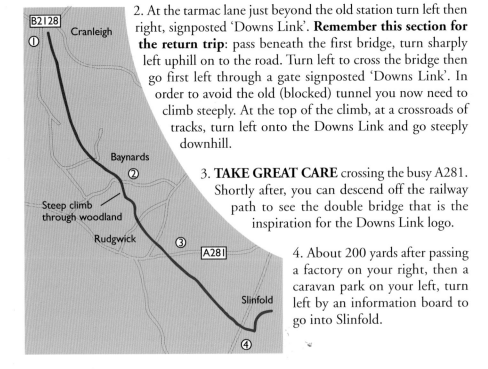

2. At the tarmac lane just beyond the old station turn left then right, signposted 'Downs Link'. **Remember this section for the return trip**: pass beneath the first bridge, turn sharply left uphill on to the road. Turn left to cross the bridge then go first left through a gate signposted 'Downs Link'. In order to avoid the old (blocked) tunnel you now need to climb steeply. At the top of the climb, at a crossroads of tracks, turn left onto the Downs Link and go steeply downhill.

3. **TAKE GREAT CARE** crossing the busy A281. Shortly after, you can descend off the railway path to see the double bridge that is the inspiration for the Downs Link logo.

4. About 200 yards after passing a factory on your right, then a caravan park on your left, turn left by an information board to go into Slinfold.

Distance: 5 miles one way, 10 miles return.

Map: Ordnance Survey Landranger map 198. A leaflet about the Downs Link can be downloaded from: www.westsussex.gov.uk and search 'Downs Link'

Hills: None.

Surface: Good stone-based tracks.

Roads and road crossings: One minor road crossing.

Refreshments: Lots of choice in Southwater. Lakeside Teas at Southwater Country Park (May to September). Partridge pub at Partridge Green.

This is the third section of the Downs Link, missing out the part between Slinfold and Southwater which is very bitty. South from Southwater the views open up with the whaleback ridge of the South Downs looming on the horizon. The suggested turn-around point is the pub at Partridge Green. If you wish to continue on you should take care along the B2135 as far as the next traffic-free section.

BACKGROUND AND PLACES OF INTEREST
Southwater Country Park
Opened in 1985 by Horsham District Council, the park offers 54 acres for informal recreation and conservation. It is open from dawn to dusk and the visitor centre is open every weekend and most days during the school holidays.

Starting Point & Parking: Lintot square, Southwater or Southwater Country Park (Grid reference TQ 160258).

ROUTE INSTRUCTIONS:
1. Start by the silver bike sculptures in Lintot Square in Southwater, by the war memorial and opposite the Lintot pub.
2. Go past Southwater Country Park, cross a minor road. Leave tarmac by a red-brick pumping station, bearing right to join the railway path.

3. Views of the South Downs open up. About 5 miles after leaving Southwater you will come across a sign for the Partridge pub in Partridge Green. If you are with children it is suggested you turn around here as the Downs Link uses a short section of the busy B2135 to the south of Partridge Green.

If you wish to continue south on the Downs Link, join the B2135, turn right, ignore the first left to the Star Trading Estate and take the next left, signposted 'Downs Link'. Tarmac turns to track. At a crossroads turn right to rejoin the railway path.

North from Southwater on the Downs Link

The Downs Link can be followed traffic-free from Southwater for 2 miles as far as Christ's Hospital School. Beyond here the route joins a busy road with a particularly dangerous right turn on a blind corner, so this is not recommended for family cycling.

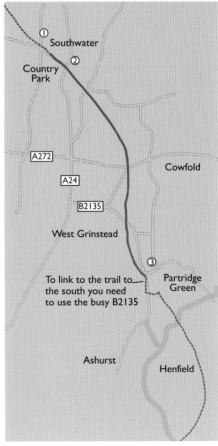

ROUTE 16
The Downs Link from Bramber to Old Shoreham or Henfield

Distance: 4½ miles one way, 9 miles return.

Map/leaflet: Ordnance Survey Landranger map 198. A leaflet about the Downs Link can be downloaded from: www.westsussex.gov.uk and search 'Downs Link' **Hills:** There are no hills south to Old Shoreham. There is a short but noticeable climb north towards Henfield.

Surface: Gravel tracks. A short section close to the river is rougher.

Roads and road crossings:

EXTREME CARE should be taken crossing the A283 south of Bramber near the start of the ride. Take plenty of time to gauge the speed of traffic before crossing, particularly if you are with young children. If you wish to miss this bit out altogether you could start from Old Shoreham and ride north as far as the A283 before turning around.

Refreshments: Bramber Castle Hotel, Old Tollgate pub, Bramber. Lots of choice in Old Shoreham. Cat & Canary pub in Henfield.

Bramber is a very attractive village at the foot of the South Downs, located on the banks of the tidal River Adur, one of only three rivers that flows south from the Weald, cutting a course through the chalk hills of the South Downs. One option runs south from Bramber alongside the river to Old Shoreham, where there is a choice of refreshment stops. There is plenty of wildlife to see along the river and fine views of Lancing College from the southern end of the ride. There is also the option of following the Downs Link north from Bramber although you should be warned that it involves some climbing so is more of a challenge for young children. **NB.** There is one busy road crossing near the start of the ride. Please take extreme care crossing the A283 just south of Bramber.

BACKGROUND AND PLACES OF INTEREST
The Downs Link
The Downs Link bridleway links the North Downs Way at St Martha's Hill near Guildford with the South Downs Way south of Steyning and follows the course of an old railway line for much of its 30-mile length. The railway fell victim to the Beeching Axe in 1966.

Bramber Castle
This National Trust property consists of the ruins of a Norman fortress built in 1083. The Civil War resulted in its destruction by Parliamentarians.

Old Shoreham
The village was stranded a mile inland when the harbour silted up in the 11th century so 'new' Shoreham was built as the new port.

Starting Point & Parking: The free car park in Bramber (Grid reference TQ187106), a village signposted off the A283 roundabout at the south end of the Steyning bypass. The ride itself starts at the roundabout with the A283 (there is a 'Downs Link' sign at the northeast corner of the roundabout).

ROUTE INSTRUCTIONS:
South of Bramber to Old Shoreham

1. Exit the car park in the centre of Bramber and turn right on the road as far as the roundabout with the A283. There is a 'Downs Link' sign immediately **before** the roundabout directing you onto a track running parallel with the southbound A283. Follow for ½ mile.

2. **TAKE EXTREME CARE** crossing the A283 to the other side. Wait patiently until there is a clear gap in the traffic for you to cross. After ¾ mile at the T-junction of tracks turn left, signposted 'South Downs Way, Eastbourne'. Cross the river bridge then turn right, signposted 'Coastal Link'.

3. Follow the track alongside the river for 3 miles, passing under a large road bridge, ignoring a wooden bridge to the right, passing under a railway bridge and alongside a new riverside development. The surface varies in quality.

4. The path ends at the Bridge Inn at the roundabout at the junction of the A283/A259 in Old Shoreham. Retrace your steps.

North of Bramber to the Cat & Canary pub, Henfield

A. Exit the car park in the centre of Bramber and turn right on the road as far as the roundabout. Immediately before the roundabout turn right onto Castle Lane. At the T-junction bear right to continue in the same direction. Shortly turn right onto King Stone Avenue.

B. At the T-junction at the end of King Stone Avenue turn right. Tarmac turns to track. Climb. At the top of the hill turn right downhill following 'Downs Link' signs.

C. Cross the river. After almost 2 miles at the T-junction with tarmac at the end of the railway path turn right. At the end of Holland Lane turn left uphill to the Cat & Canary pub. It is suggested you turn around here.

If you wish to continue further north on the Downs Link, after about 2 miles of railway path you will need to spend about ½ mile on the busy B2135 through Partridge Green before rejoining the traffic-free path.

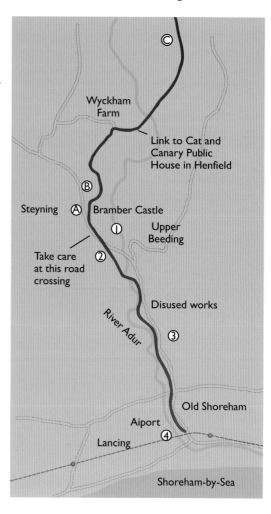

Distance: 6 miles one way, 12 miles return.

Map: Ordnance Survey Landranger map 198.

Hills: There is a climb up from the promenade near the marina to the cliffs running east to Rottingdean.

Surface: Concrete tracks or tarmac.

Roads and road crossings: There are several road crossings and quiet streets are used at the eastern end close to the marina.

Refreshments:
Lots of choice all along the seafront and in Rottingdean.

Ever more seaside resorts in the South of England are creating cycle paths along the wide promenades that run parallel with the coast, offering cyclists the chance to glide along from one end of a resort to the other with fine views out to sea and myriad opportunities to stop for refreshments. The route through Brighton passes the famous Brighton Pier and continues on to Rottingdean where you have the option of a high level route along the cliff top or a route at sea level right beneath the towering chalk cliffs. Why not go out on one option and return on the other?

NB Please ride responsibly along the promenade, especially during busy summer weekends: pay attention to the cycling signs and be aware that the paths are shared with pedestrians.

Starting Points & Parking: If you live in the Brighton/Hove area the seafront cycle path can be joined at any point between Hove Lagoon and Brighton Marina. If you are arriving by car from outside the area, parking in central Brighton can be very expensive. It would be better either to start from Rottingdean in the east or to park at the Southwick Bay car park/Carat Cafe near Shoreham docks at the western end of the spit of land beyond Portslade-by-Sea (Grid reference TQ 243047).

ROUTE INSTRUCTIONS:
West to east from Hove Lagoon

1. The route is well waymarked as National Cycle Network Route 2. Signs on the ground, painted cycle lanes and 'No Cycling' signs will all give you a clear indication of the course of the route, at times right by the seafront, at other times set back from it.

2. Go past Brighton Pier and towards the marina. The route climbs up away from the seafront. At the top of the climb you have a choice:

(a) bear left through the subway under the A259 to join the clifftop path past the windmill to Rottingdean to finish at the White Horse Hotel.

(b) bear right downhill to join the Undercliff Path running beneath the towering chalk cliffs on a wide concrete path that also leads to Rottingdean.

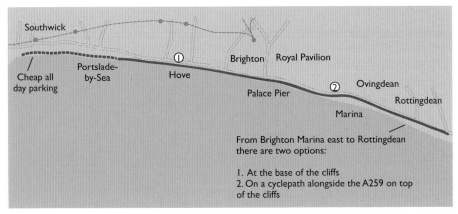

Southwick

Cheap all
day parking

Portslade-
by-Sea

① Hove

Brighton / Royal Pavilion

Palace Pier

② Ovingdean

Marina

Rottingdean

From Brighton Marina east to Rottingdean there are two options:

1. At the base of the cliffs
2. On a cyclepath alongside the A259 on top of the cliffs

ROUTE 18

Worth Way, between Crawley and East Grinstead

Distance: 6 miles one way, 12 miles return.

Map: Ordnance Survey Landranger map 187.

Website: www.westsussex.gov.uk and search 'Worth Way'. **Hills:** None.

Surface: Good stone-based tracks, tarmac.

Roads and road crossings:

Several minor roads are crossed and quiet residential roads are used for about ¾ mile through Crawley Down. If you wish to connect to the Forest Way, another railway path starting on the east side of East Grinstead, you will need to go through the town centre.

Refreshments: Royal Oak pub, Crawley Down. Lots of choice in East Grinstead.

Lying on the course of National Cycle Network Route 21 which links London to the South Coast, the Worth Way is one of two railway paths that start in East Grinstead. This one begins from the back of the railway station and almost immediately you are rolling along a smooth broad track through mature broadleaf woodland beneath a series of fine brick bridges. There is a short section on residential roads through Crawley Down before rejoining the traffic-free railway path as far as Worth where you may choose to visit the splendid church.

BACKGROUND AND PLACES OF INTEREST

History of the railway path

Opened in 1979 and now forming a valuable wildlife corridor, the Worth Way follows the course of the old railway branch line which ran from East Grinstead to Three Bridges between 1855 and 1967. Many birds such as nuthatch, chiffchaff and Great tit can be seen in the trees and scrub. In the more open area plants such as primrose and common spotted orchid may be found, while speckled wood butterflies can be seen in the sunny glades.

Starting Point & Parking:

1. Worth Church signposted just off the B2036 on the east side of Crawley, close to Junction 10 or 10a of the M23 (Grid reference TQ 302364).

2. East Grinstead railway station car park (Grid reference TQ 388383). If this is full there is another car park on Railway Approach, about ½ mile east of the railway station.

ROUTE INSTRUCTIONS:

1. The trail starts by a 'Worth Way' signboard about 100 yards before Worth Church.

2. After 1¼ miles cross the road by Keepers Cottage. Follow the railway path for 2 miles.

3. Join a residential road. The route is well signposted through Crawley Down as 'Worth Way' or 'National Cycle Network Route 21'. At the offset crossroads at the end of Old Station Close turn left, then right onto Burleigh Way. Ignore Copse Close and take the next right on Woodland Drive. Shortly turn left onto Hazel Way then right onto Cob Close.

4. Rejoin the old railway line. Go past Crawley Down Pond and follow for 2 miles to finish at East Grinstead railway station car park.

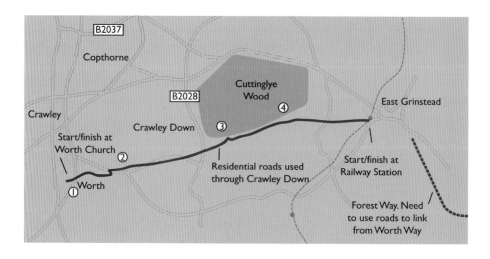

Distance: 10 miles one way, 20 miles return.

Map: Ordnance Survey Landranger maps 187 and 188.

Website:www.eastsussex.gov.uk/leisureandtourism/countryside/walks/forestway

Hills: Short climb on road at the start in Groombridge. Gentle climb from Forest Row up to East Grinstead.

Surface: Good stone-based tracks, tarmac.

Roads and road crossings: A short section of minor road is used from the car park in Groombridge to the start of the traffic-free trail. Several minor road crossings. The busy A22 to the north of Forest Row is crossed via a toucan crossing. If you wish to go into East Grinstead for refreshments (or to link to the Worth Way) you will need to use streets.

Refreshments: Crown pub, Junction Inn, Groombridge. Lots of choice in East Grinstead. Pubs off the route in Hartfield and Forest Row.

Running west from Groombridge to East Grinstead, this railway path offers an easy ride on a broad stone-based track ideal for side-by-side conversation, passing through a mix of broadleaf woodland and open arable countryside. There are pubs and a bakery in Groombridge and plenty of choice in East Grinstead, giving you a target to aim for whether you are starting from the east or the west.

BACKGROUND AND PLACES OF INTEREST

History of the railway path

Passing through the High Weald Area of Outstanding Natural Beauty, the route follows the course of the old East Grinstead, Groombridge & Tunbridge Wells Railway line, which opened in 1866 and closed in 1967 as part of the reforms proposed by Dr Beeching, who lived alongside the railway at East Grinstead.

Trees and Wildlife

Alder and willow abound in the fields on either side of the line because of its location in the floodplain of the River Medway: these trees like the wet ground and large areas of the surrounding countryside can be flooded for weeks at a time.

The river also attracts birds: look out for mallard, moorhens and herons.

Starting Points & Parking:

1. Groombridge – there is a free car park by the Post Office and bakery (Grid reference TQ 531373).

2. East Grinstead – the trail starts at the east end of the High Street, at the junction of Lewes Road (B2110) with Old Road by the roundabout with the A22 (Grid reference TQ 401379). The nearest car park is on De La Warr Road, off College Lane (B2110).

ROUTE INSTRUCTIONS:

1. Follow Corseley Road from the Post Office in Groombridge, climbing and ignoring several rights and lefts. The road swings

left at the top of the climb then **(easy to miss)** on the descent, immediately before the pumping station, turn right onto a gravel track signposted 'Hartfield 3½, Forest Row 8, National Cycle Network Route 21'.

2. Cross several (minor) roads on a continuation of the railway path, passing through woodland or arable farmland.

3. Follow signs carefully at the western end of Forest Row past a red-brick pumping station. Cross the busy A22 via a toucan crossing.

4. At a fork of two uphill paths shortly after a road crossing on the eastern edge of East Grinstead bear left to emerge at the High Street/Old Road in East Grinstead.

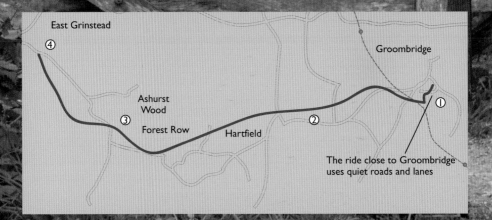

ROUTE 20
Tonbridge to Penshurst Place

Distance: 5 miles one way, 10 miles return.

Map: Ordnance Survey Landranger map 188. A *Tonbridge Castle to Penshurst Place Map & Guide* is available from Tonbridge Tourist Information Centre (01732 770929) or can be downloaded from: www.sevenoaks.gov.uk/-documents/tonbridgeleaflet.pdf

Hills: One steady climb from the Ensfield Road up to Well Place Farm.

Surface: Good stone-based tracks, tarmac.

Roads and road crossings: A short section of road is used through Lower Haysden and again on Ensfield Road at the crossing of the River Medway.

Refreshments: Lots of choice in Tonbridge. If you wish to use the tearooms at Penshurst Place you will need to pay the entrance fee to visit the building.

The bike route between Tonbridge Castle and Penshurst Place offers an excellent, almost entirely traffic-free ride from the heart of Tonbridge alongside the River Medway, out into the countryside as far as the glorious buildings of Penshurst Place, some five miles to the west. The ride takes you past playing fields on the edge of Tonbridge and into Haysden Country Park, running around the edge of Barden Lake with its wide variety of birdlife. Shortly after passing beneath the A21 you enter a delightful secret kingdom of lush broadleaf woodland carpeted with wildflowers in the spring and a delight in autumn as the colours change. The one noticeable climb of the day comes between the bridge over the River Medway and Well Place Farm,

giving you wide-ranging views of the surrounding countryside and setting you up for a fine descent past two lakes to arrive at Penshurst Place, the finest and most complete example in England of 14th-century domestic architecture.

Starting Point & Parking:
Tonbridge Swimming Pool car park, near the castle (Grid reference TQ 590466)

ROUTE INSTRUCTIONS:

1. From the entrance to Tonbridge Swimming Pool car park, by a 'Children' road sign, take the access road to the overflow car park, keeping the rugby clubhouse to your left. The cycle path starts at the end of the overflow car park, running around the edge of the playing fields. Follow National Cycle Network Route 12 signs into woodland and over a series of bridges with metal railings.

2. Emerge at Barden Lake, turn left and keep the water to your right. At the end of the lake turn left to go under a railway bridge then at the T-junction, with the car park to the right, turn left. At the next T-junction, at the end of the approach road to Haysden Country Park, turn right, signposted 'Penshurst Bike Route'.

3. Follow this lane through the village of Lower Haysden, past the pub, under the A21, turn first right, then left onto a stone track signposted 'Public Bridleway'. Follow the excellently signposted track through lovely broadleaf woodland.

4. At the end of the track, at the T-junction with a road, turn right then shortly after crossing the bridge take the first concrete track to the left, signposted 'Penshurst 1½'.

5. Climb on this broad concrete track then descend past Well Place Farm towards the magnificent buildings of Penshurst Place.

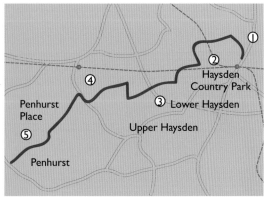

Distance: 12½-mile circuit.

Map: Ordnance Survey Landranger map 188. A map is also available at the Visitor Centre.

Website: www.bewl.co.uk

Hills: Several short climbs and descents.

Surface: Varied. There are sections of tarmac, good gravel track and firm earth track but also some rough, rutted and at times muddy stretches. Avoid after prolonged rain. It is closed in winter.

Roads and road crossings: The lanes that are used are very quiet as they are not through roads and carry almost no traffic.

Refreshments: At the Visitor Centre. The Bull pub at Three Leg Cross is on the far side of the lake from the Visitor Centre, about halfway around the circuit.

Cycle Hire: Bewl Bike Hire 01892 891446 (closed in winter).

A circular route around the largest reservoir in the South East. This is one of the few circular rides in the book and the setting is lovely. However, compared to cycle trails around other reservoirs in the country, the standard of the surface is much rougher and is actually shut during the winter. For maximum enjoyment it is best to choose a fine day after a dry spell and to use mountain bikes with suspension.

BACKGROUND AND PLACES OF INTEREST

Around the lake

The dam is made from local clay faced with concrete slabs to prevent erosion and holds back 6,900 million gallons of water. The tall draw-off tower controls water abstraction. Nearby Chingley Wood is a mixed coppice woodland once used for fuelling ironworks in the valley. Several willow plantations around the lake produce timber for the manufacture of cricket bats.

Lamberhurst

An ancient centre of the local iron industry. Now a vineyard grows beside the village green. There are ingenious displays in Heaver's Model Museum and Craft Centre in a converted oast house. Smugglers used Owl House and warned of approaching excisemen by hooting.

Scotney Castle (1 mile north of Bewl Water)

The moated ruins of the 14th century castle are set among romantic landscaped gardens filled with roses and flowering shrubs.

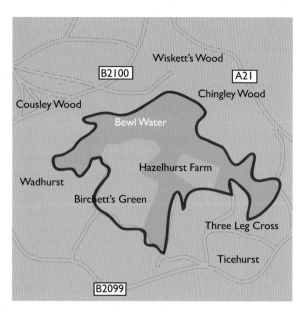

Starting Point & Parking:
The Visitor Centre is located near Lamberhurst, off the A21 between Tunbridge Wells and Hastings (Grid reference TQ 676338). There is a £6 charge for the car park.

ROUTE INSTRUCTIONS:
The route starts from the back of the brick building housing the cafe, opposite the terrace. Head towards the dam to pick up the signs. The route is waymarked with 'Round Water Route' signs but sometimes these are hard to see. Quiet lanes are used for 2½ miles on the southern side of the lake.

ROUTE 22
Bedgebury Forest, southwest of Cranbrook

Distance: 5-mile circuit.

Map: Ordnance Survey Landranger map 188. A *Bedgebury Trail Map* is available from the Visitor Centre (01580 879820).

Website: www.forestry.gov.uk/bedgebury

Hills: There are several hills. The toughest is right at the start and younger children may prefer to walk.

Surface: Good quality gravel tracks.

Roads and road crossings: There are no roads or road crossings.

Refreshments: There is a cafe at the Visitor Centre.

Cycle Hire: Quench Cycles (01580 879694) or go to their website: www.quenchuk.co.uk

Bedgebury Forest is the only Forestry Commission holding in Kent with waymarked bike routes. There is a 5-mile circuit aimed at families and an 8-mile, tougher single-track course for more experienced mountain bikers. Bedgebury is mixed woodland and in amongst the fir and conifers you will find sweet chestnut, birch, oak and sycamore, not to mention bright yellow ragwort, purple willowherb and foxgloves. The forest lies adjacent to Bedgebury Pinetum, which contains a magnificent collection of rare trees and flowering shrubs. There is a lovely picnic spot by the lakes that you pass along the route.

NB There is a £7 charge to use the car park. This goes down to £3 for visits after 1700hrs.

BACKGROUND AND PLACES OF INTEREST
Bedgebury Pinetum
With nearly 10,000 trees and shrubs the National Pinetum is the most complete collection of temperate conifers in the world. The collection was started in the 1840s by the Beresford Hope family. The Pinetum was taken over by the Forestry Commission in 1925. The Great Storm of 1987 destroyed thirty per cent of the trees but allowed massive replanting to achieve a better balance of coniferous trees, broadleaf trees and open spaces.

Starting Point & Parking: Off the B2079 about 1 mile north of its junction with the A21 between Lamberhurst and Hastings (Grid reference TQ 715336).

ROUTE INSTRUCTIONS:

The route is well signposted with marker posts 1-63. The only choice you have to make is whether to do it clockwise, following the numbers in ascending order, or anti-clockwise, following the numbers down from 63 to 1. Louisa Lake is about halfway around the circuit.

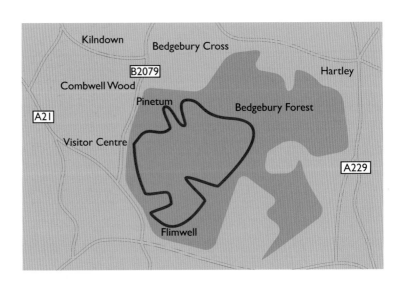

Distance: 11 miles one way, 22 miles return.

Map: Ordnance Survey Landranger map 199.

Website: www.eastsussex.gov.uk and search 'Cuckoo Trail map'

Hills: There is a gentle climb from Polegate up to Heathfield, more pronounced at the northern end of the ride. Bear this in mind if setting off from Heathfield.

Surface: Tarmac.

Roads and road crossings: Several road crossings (the busy roads have toucan crossings). Residential streets are used in Horam and Hailsham.

Refreshments: Lots of choice in Heathfield, Horam, Hailsham and Polegate. The Old Loom Mill tearoom lies 50 yards off the trail about 1 mile north of Polegate (signposted on the east side of the path).

The Cuckoo Trail is the most popular railway path in Southeast England, offering 11 miles of superb traffic-free cycling in the heart of beautiful Sussex with fine views south towards the chalk ridge of the South Downs. There is plenty of interest with wooden sculptures, a metal pagoda, and information boards about wildlife. It is a gentle descent from Heathfield for the first five miles so be aware of this if you start here as there may be some tired legs at the end of your return journey. There are a couple of places where the railway line has been built over and you need to use residential roads but these are all well signposted. The trail is a delight all year round but especially so in spring with carpets of bluebells on the woodland floor and in late autumn with the changing colours.

Starting Points & Parking:

There are car parks that are convenient for the Cuckoo Trail in:

1. Heathfield at the junction of Station Road and Newnham Way, to the south of the High Street (A265) (Grid reference TQ 582213).

2. Horam near the junction of the B2203 and Hillside Drive (Grid reference TQ 578175).

3. Hailsham at the junction of Station Road and the A295 (Grid reference TQ 589093).

ROUTE INSTRUCTIONS:

1. From the Heathfield car park follow the Cuckoo Trail southwards, crossing a couple of minor roads before joining the old railway path.

2. Long gentle descent over several miles.

3. In Hailsham pay close attention to the signs as you need to use residential roads through the town. Make sure you are following the Cuckoo Trail for cyclists, not the route for walkers or horses.

4. The route ends in Polegate. You may wish to go into the town or simply turn around at this point. Be aware that there is a gentle climb back up to Heathfield.

ROUTE 24
Friston Forest, west of Eastbourne

Distance: 5-mile circuit.

Map: Ordnance Survey Landranger map 199. Of more use is the free *Friston Forest* leaflet available at the Visitor Centre.

Hills: Two noticeable climbs.

Surface: Good stone-based tracks, with occasional puddles after rain.

Roads and road crossings: None

Refreshments: Tearoom near the Visitor Centre.

There are two waymarked trails in Friston Forest: a 5-mile circuit mainly on wide forest roads aimed at families and novices and a tougher 7-mile single-track course, the Jeremy Cole Mountain Bike Trail, for more experienced mountain bikers. It is also possible to cycle on the broad track south from the Visitor Centre through Seven Sisters Country Park down to the sea at Cuckmere Haven, although this will involve crossing the busy A259 on the way there and back. The trail in Friston Forest is not flat but what goes up must come down and there is a fun, grassy descent towards the end of the ride.

BACKGROUND AND PLACES OF INTEREST

Friston Forest

In 1880, the Eastbourne Water Company bought a large area of downland west of Eastbourne in order to use the water resource held within the chalk as the supply for Eastbourne. During the 1920s the company granted approximately 2000 acres to the Forestry Commission on a long-term lease in order to create a forest that would help protect the water supply below. Today it is a mature, mainly broadleaved beech forest.

Starting Point & Parking:

Car park near the Friston Forest/Seven Sisters Country Park Visitor Centre, on the minor road towards Litlington, just off the A259, about 6 miles west of Eastbourne (Grid reference TV 519995).

ROUTE INSTRUCTIONS:

1. From the car park by the Visitor Centre go back towards the exit then turn right at a square wooden post signposted 'Bridleway to West Dean,' soon joining the family cycle trail at a large green and white 'Friston Forest' sign.

2. At the track junction with brick and flint Pond Cottage ahead bear right to join a better gravel track. Follow this long, wide, straight forest road, passing flint houses on left and going round a metal barrier across the road. At the crossroads of wide tracks by tall red and white poles go straight ahead.

3. After almost ½ mile the path narrows, then swings left and starts climbing. Shortly turn left uphill off the wide gravel track onto a stone and earth track, soon turning left again (all signposted).

4. Long gentle descent on earth and grass track. At a crossroads with smooth forest road turn right gently uphill. After ¼ mile turn left on a similar broad forest road. Climb to the highpoint with the option of turning right up to the viewpoint (rough and steep). For the main route continue straight ahead downhill.

5. At the T-junction with a forest road at the bottom of a fun, grassy descent turn right to rejoin the outward route back to the start.

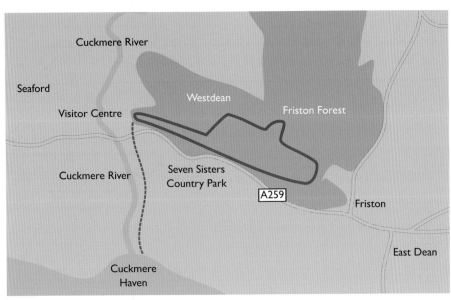

Distance: East to Folkestone – 5 miles one way, 10 miles return.
West along the Military Canal – 1½ miles one way, 3 miles return.

Map: Ordnance Survey Landranger map 179.

Hills: None.

Surface: Tarmac or concrete seafront promenade heading east from Hythe.
Short stone and gravel section on the canal towpath heading west.

Roads and road crossings: Several road crossings. You will need to use streets
to go into the centre of Folkestone.

Refreshments: Lots of choice in Hythe and Folkestone.

This is surely one of the finest seafront cycle routes on the English South Coast. Other cycling promenades such as Bournemouth or Brighton may be full of things to see but they are also very popular with pedestrians and much of your time is spent looking out for other people. Here, for much of the time you can enjoy the views out over the English Channel without fear of the crowds. There are two very contrasting ways of extending this ride: continuing east along National Cycle Network Route 2 you will be faced with a climb of almost 600 ft up onto the famous white cliffs between Folkestone and Dover; to the west the Military Canal leads to the amazing network of quiet flat lanes that criss-cross Romney Marsh, an area as flat as the Somerset Levels or the Fenland of East Anglia.

BACKGROUND AND PLACES OF INTEREST

Hythe

The town is one of the original Cinque Ports (Hastings, New Romney, Hythe, Dover and Sandwich); at a later date Rye and Winchelsea were also added. In return for certain privileges and trading concessions, the Cinque Ports were obliged to give Ship Service, providing ships for the king's use as a protection force for the coast before the establishment of the Royal Navy in the 15th century.

The Royal Military Canal

The canal was built between 1804 and 1809 for strategic defence against invasion in the Napoleonic Wars with France. It runs for 28 miles from Seabrook (near Folkestone) to Cliff End (near Hastings).

Starting Point & Parking:

There is a free car park at the back of the Dukes Head pub, on Portland Road, off the A259 Dymchurch Road in the centre of Hythe, near the junction with the A261 (Grid reference TR 147137).

ROUTE INSTRUCTIONS:
East from Hythe to Folkestone

1. From the car park at the back of the Dukes Head pub (Portland Road) drop down to join the canal towpath and turn right (i.e. keep the water to your left), following National Cycle Network Route 2 signs.

2. At the end of Portland Road cross Stade Street onto a tarmac drive alongside the canal. Shortly, opposite a blue metal bridge on the left, turn right onto Ladies Walk (NCN 2) by the Hythe Bowling Club. Cross the road onto Moyle Tower Road to join the wide red tarmac promenade. Turn left.

3. Absolutely fabulous promenade: red tarmac turns to white concrete. The trail ends just before the docks, bearing left away from the sea to the fringe of woodland and following residential roads into Folkestone. You may prefer to turn around and return to Hythe.

West from Hythe along Royal Military Canal
Heading west from the Dukes Head pub in Hythe, the Military Canal can be followed for approximately 1.5 miles through parkland then along Green Lane as far as a metal bridge which drops you opposite Peregrine Close (and then a further 1.5 miles on a quiet road for refreshments at the Botolphs Bridge Inn or the chance to explore the quiet flat lane network of Romney Marsh).

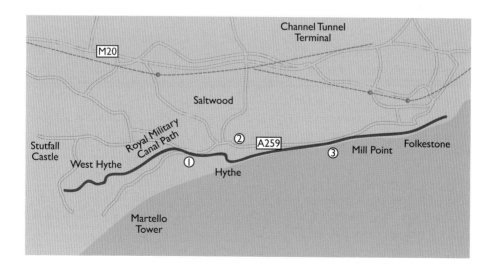

ROUTE 26

The Chalk & Channel Way between Folkestone and Dover

Distance: 5 miles one way, 10 miles return.

Map: Ordnance Survey Landranger map 179. A *Chalk & Channel Way* leaflet is available from Sustrans (www.sustrans.org.uk).

Hills: The ride along the top is gently undulating. If you start from the centres of either Dover or Folkestone you will be faced with a long steep climb.

Surface: Stone-based tracks, gravel tracks or tarmac cycle paths.

Roads and road crossings: There are several sections of quiet roads used and one crossing of a busier road (the B2011) if you choose to explore to the west towards Folkestone.

Refreshments: Cliff Top Cafe at the start. Lighthouse Inn, about 1 mile east of Capel-le-Ferne. Valiant Sailor pub on the B2011 west of Old Dover Road.

On a fine, clear day the views across to France from the top of the cliffs between Folkestone and Dover are quite extraordinary. It is a superb airy ride high up above the English Channel with some interesting artworks along the way. As it is a climb of over 500 ft up from Folkestone or from Dover, the suggested starting point is on the top of the cliffs above Folkestone. Samphire Hoe was created from the chalk that was excavated from under the sea to create the Channel Tunnel. It is already beginning to grass over and there is a circular ride around this new piece of England.

Starting Point & Parking: Old Dover Road, Capel-le-Ferne, between Folkestone and Dover. Turn off the B2011 just east of the Battle of Britain memorial (Grid reference TR 246383).

ROUTE INSTRUCTIONS:

East towards Dover

1. From the Cliff Top Cafe follow the road east towards Dover (with the sea to your right).

2. Go past the Lighthouse Inn and join a cycle path alongside the B2011. After about ¼ mile bear right, soon joining a superb gravel path along the cliff top.

3. After 2½ miles the path emerges alongside the A20. Here you have three choices:

(a) turn back

(b) continue on into Dover, bearing in mind that after crossing the footbridge over the A20 the rest of the route is a long descent on residential streets or cycle paths alongside busier roads

(c) drop down to the right to explore the cycle paths on Samphire Hoe

West towards Folkestone

From the Cliff Top Cafe it is possible to go west for about 1 mile on the Chalk & Channel Way while still maintaining your height, offering fine views out over the channel. Turn left on the cycle path along the B2011 then bear right onto Crete Road. This can be followed for 1 mile to its junction with the A260, north of Folkestone.

NB National Cycle Network Route 2 drops over 550 ft from the cliffs down to the sea at Folkestone (via residential streets) so the climb back up from here should only be undertaken by fit cyclists.

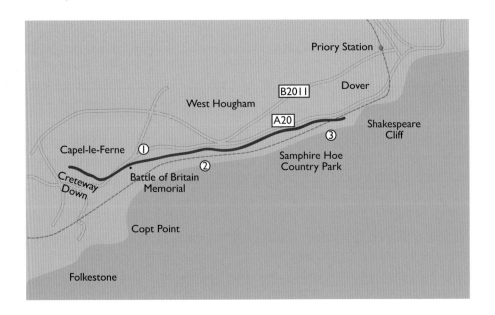

Distance: 6 miles one way, 12 miles return.

Map: Ordnance Survey Landranger map 179.

Hills: Steady climb up from the coast at Oldstairs Bay to St Margaret's.

Surface: Good stone-based tracks or tarmac.

Roads and road crossings: There are two short sections on quiet residential roads – the first through Kingsdown and the second at the end of the ride to reach the pub in St Margaret's.

Refreshments: Lots of choice in Deal. Red Lion pub in St Margaret's.

Starting from the attractive town of Deal with its brightly coloured seafront houses, its pier and castle, this ride runs traffic-free alongside the shingle beach covered in lobster pots and fishing boats. After briefly turning inland in Kingsdown (where there is a short section on road), you return to the sea at Oldstairs Bay before the long steady climb up from the coast to the pub at St Margaret's. You deserve your refreshments and can now look forward to a long gentle descent back down to the coast.

BACKGROUND AND PLACES OF INTEREST

Deal Castle

Henry VIII built a castle in the shape of a six-leaf clover (or a Tudor Rose) at Deal, although natural protection already existed in the form of the Goodwin Sands. These huge shifting beds lie five miles offshore and have caused hundreds of wrecks. It is among the earliest and most elaborate of a chain of coastal forts that were built to protect England's South Coast from invasion by European Catholic powers.

Walmer Castle

Another castle built by Henry VIII, this one is the official residence of the Lord Warden of the Cinque Ports. The Duke of Wellington died here and a number of his possessions are on display inside.

Starting Point & Parking: The pier in Deal (Grid reference TR 378526). There are several Pay & Display car parks in the town.

ROUTE INSTRUCTIONS:

1. The traffic-free promenade starts just south of the pier in Deal by a roundabout with a telephone box in it. Follow the signposted cycle path alongside a shingle beach with the sea to your left.

2. After 2 miles, at the end of the promenade, follow the pavement of the unmade residential road, following the road round to the right after ½ mile.

3. At the T-junction with a busier road turn left for ¼ mile past Kitty's Tearoom and the Rising Sun pub, soon bearing left onto Cliffe Road, following NCN 1 signs.

4. After ½ mile follow Oldstairs Road round to the right away from the beach then keep an eye out for a right turn signposted 'Kingsdown Riding Centre, National Cycle Network Route 1'.

5. Long steady climb on tarmac cycle path then residential road to the Red Lion pub on Kingsdown Road in St Margaret's. Beyond this point National Cycle Network Route 1 joins busier roads and drops down into Dover.

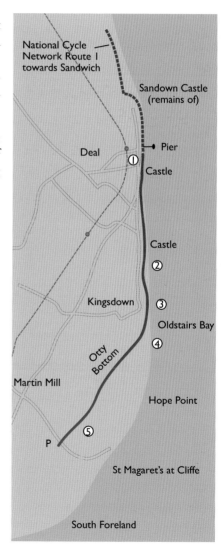

National Cycle Network Route 1 towards Sandwich

Sandown Castle (remains of)

Deal — Pier

① Castle

Castle

②

Kingsdown ③

Oldstairs Bay

④

Otty Bottom

Martin Mill

Hope Point

P ⑤

St Magaret's at Cliffe

South Foreland

ROUTE 28
Reculver to Margate along the Kent Coast

Distance: 9 miles one way, 18 miles return.

Map: Ordnance Survey Landranger map 179. You can download the Viking Coastal Trail leaflet at www.visitthanet.co.uk/viking

Website: www.vikingcoastaltrail.co.uk

Hills: None.

Surface: Good stone-based tracks or tarmac.

Roads and road crossings: Occasional short sections of road from Minnis Bay east through Westgate on Sea to Margate.

Refreshments: King Ethelbert pub, Reculver. Lots of choice from Minnis Bay eastwards to Margate.

Bike hire: At the seafront car park in Minnis Bay (07772 037609).

The Viking Coastal Trail is the name given to a 27-mile ride around the shoreline of the Isle of Thanet, at the north-eastern tip of the coast of Kent. It is a mixture of traffic-free trails, quiet roads and traffic-calmed streets in the coastal towns. The section from Reculver to Margate is the one with the highest traffic-free proportion. It starts from the distinctive towers of the ruins of Reculver Church and proceeds east along a wide concrete sea wall with a shingle beach to your left with many breakwaters made of huge boulders; away to the right are flat fertile fields dedicated to arable farming. Coastal resorts at Birchington and Westgate are interspersed with sandy bays. Shingle beaches turn to low chalk cliffs and before long you can sample the delights of Margate.

NB In the Margate area there are several short sections where cyclists must dismount in front of the rows of the beach huts between 1000-1800 hrs from May to September. Young children might easily run out of the huts or cross without looking from the beach back to the huts, hence the need for this measure.

BACKGROUND AND PLACES OF INTEREST
The Isle of Thanet
The Wantsum Channel from Reculver to Pegwell Bay was once an open waterway separating the Isle of Thanet from mainland Kent. During the Roman period it was more than half a mile wide in places. The channel slowly silted up with final closure of the northern end occurring when the Northern Sea Wall was constructed across the mouth at Coldharbour.

Starting Point & Parking: Reculver Country Park car park by the King Ethelbert pub and the church ruins in Reculver, on the north Kent coast, to the east of Herne Bay (Grid reference TR 226693).

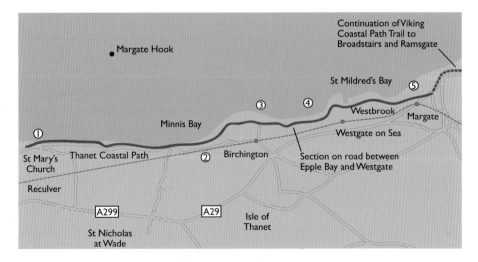

ROUTE INSTRUCTIONS:

1. The route is signposted as the Viking Trail from Reculver on a wide concrete path along the sea wall.

2. After almost 4 miles, this first traffic-free section ends in a car park near Minnis Bay. Go around the edge of the car park, descend to the promenade and turn right (follow signs).

3. Go past a series of low chalk cliffs. Almost 2 miles after the car park and about 200 yards before the end of the path (there are steps ahead with railings), keep an eye out for a right turn uphill on a cobbled path cut through the chalk.

4. Follow the cycle lane on the road for almost 1 mile then descend back down to the promenade. Please **dismount** in front of the beach huts as indicated by the signs.

5. The trail leads into the heart of Margate where you may turn around after finding some refreshments or continue along the Viking Coastal Trail (which has more road sections beyond this point) to North Foreland, Broadstairs and Ramsgate.

ROUTE 29
Crab and Winkle Way, from Canterbury to Whitstable

Distance: 8 miles one way, 16 miles return. The longest traffic-free section is between the University of Kent and South Street (on the south side of Whitstable).

Map: Ordnance Survey Landranger map 179. A *Crab & Winkle Way* leaflet is available from Tourist Information Centres or go to www.kent.gov.uk, put 'Crab & Winkle Way' into the 'Search' box and follow links.

Hills: Steady climb from the centre of Canterbury to the University of Kent.

Surface: Good stone-based tracks or tarmac.

Roads and road crossings: There are several sections of quiet residential roads used between the start in the centre of Canterbury and the University of Kent then from South Street to the harbour in Whitstable.

Refreshments: Lots of choice in Canterbury and Whitstable. Nothing in between.

This ride links the stunning historic centre of Canterbury with the coast at Whitstable via a mixture of cycle paths, quiet residential roads and traffic-free sections through woodland and arable land. The ride climbs gently from West Gate, part of Canterbury's city walls, up to the University of Kent, offering fine views back down over the city and the towers of the cathedral. On the long traffic-free section north from here you pass a great variety of Kent's agricultural produce, from cereal crops to fruit orchards and glass houses with tomatoes and soft fruit. The woodland section is a riot of wild flowers in spring and summer with bluebells, campion, cow parsley, buttercup and stitchwort among the most common. The route reaches a highpoint and descends on a mixture of quiet roads and cycle paths down to the harbour at Whitstable and a chance to sample the local seafood.

HISTORY AND PLACES OF INTEREST

The railway line

The Crab & Winkle Way takes its name from the railway line which ran between Canterbury and Whitstable. The line started operating in 1830 and was the first regular steam passenger service in the world. George Stephenson and his son Robert engineered the line and the original engine, the *Invicta*, which was based on the famous *Rocket*. The *Invicta* could only be used for the first part of the journey because it did not have enough power to haul carriages up the gradients. Two winding engines did this job, one at the halt on Tyler Hill Road and one in Clowes Wood. The line operated as a passenger railway until 1932 and for freight until 1952. Parts of it were reopened as a cycle route in 1999.

Starting Point & Parking: West Gate, at the western end of St Peter Street in the centre of Canterbury (Grid reference TR 146581).

ROUTE INSTRUCTIONS:

1. Follow 'Crab & Winkle', 'National Cycle Network Route 1', 'University' or 'Whitstable' signs from West Gate along Westgate Grove alongside the river. The route is well signposted along connecting cycle paths or cycle lanes on the following quiet roads: Whitehall Road, Whitehall Bridge Road, Queens Avenue, Fisher Road and Westgate Court Avenue.

2. Climb gently. A longer traffic-free section on a narrow tarmac path around or between fields with views back down to Canterbury leads towards a large round white water tower with masts.

3. At the T-junction with the A290 at the end of Neals Place Road turn left, then at the toucan crossing after ¼ mile (near Kent College) cross to the cycle path

on the other side, soon bearing right onto a stone track signposted 'Crab & Winkle'. Join the start of the main traffic-free section by the University of Kent car park.

4. Descend on tarmac and climb on a fine gravel path past a church on the left. Shortly cross a road. Go past arable fields and orchards and into woodland. At a T-junction turn right then shortly at the next T-junction turn left, signposted 'Whitstable 3½', briefly joining the course of the old railway.

5. Long gentle descent, short climb. At the fork bear left. At the end of the traffic-free path join a busier road for ¼ mile then at a metal penny farthing sculpture just beyond Millstrood Road bear left onto a cycle path (Invicta Way).

6. Closely follow signs along All Saints Close, Seymour Avenue, past Whitstable railway station, along Stream Walk and Albert Street to arrive in the centre of Whitstable.

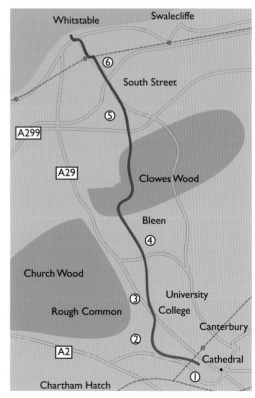

ROUTE 30
Greenwich to the Thames Barrier and Erith

Distance: 13 miles one way, 26 miles return.

Map: Ordnance Survey Landranger map 177. A street map of London would be just as helpful or the Transport for London Cycle Guides: see www.tfl.gov.uk/cycling.

Hills: None.

Surface: Tarmac or good stone-based tracks with one or two rougher sections close to Greenwich.

Roads and road crossings: Several road crossings and two sections where you are diverted away from the river onto parallel roads – the first is just east of Greenwich and the other is between the Thames Flood Barrier and Woolwich.

Refreshments: Lots of choice in Greenwich, Woolwich and Erith. Otherwise you will need a street map to navigate your way from the river then back again.

Earlier in the book Ride 5 explores the River Thames as it enters London from the west; this ride shows a very different face of the river as it approaches the final part of its journey to the sea. Starting in Greenwich, site of the Cutty Sark and the splendour of the Royal Naval College, the ride weaves its way through the streets to emerge beneath the O2 Arena (what was originally the Millennium Dome). The silver shell structures of the Thames Barrier offer another memorable landmark. Beyond here there is a short unavoidable section on road before rejoining the river near the Woolwich Ferry. East of here the character of the river is dominated by the shipping of sand and gravel. It is a wide commercial waterway,

far removed from the pleasure boats and wooded banks of the Thames to the west of the city. There is plenty to see along the way, from metal sculptures to old wooden wharfs. The trail improves as it goes further east, becoming a wide smooth concrete path leading to Erith where you have several options (see below).

BACKGROUND AND PLACES OF INTEREST

Crossness Pumping Station

Constructed as part of Victorian London's new sewage disposal system in the fight against diseases like cholera, the station opened in 1865 and houses four steam-powered beam engines believed to be the largest surviving of their kind in the world.

Birdlife

Twice a day the tide drops around 20ft, exposing mud rich in shellfish and worms. This attracts thousands of birds, some resident and some choosing to rest on their long migratory journeys. The estuaries along the Thames are vital links in the East Atlantic Flyway, a chain of bird migration sites stretching from the Arctic to Africa.

Starting Points & Parking:

1. Greenwich – the Cutty Sark/the dome for the Greenwich Foot Tunnel in Greenwich, east London (Grid reference TQ 383779).

2. Erith train station, east along the Thames towards Dartford (Grid reference TQ 512782).

ROUTE INSTRUCTIONS:

1. The route between Greenwich and the O2 Arena (was The Dome) does not lie right by the river so you will need to follow 'Thames Cycle Route/National Cycle Network Route 1' signs closely.

2. Pass around the peninsula beneath the outside of the Dome/O2 Arena.

3. Follow close to the river as far as the distinctive silver structures of the Thames Flood Barrier. At this point you will once again need to leave the river on a well signposted route along residential streets (and on a cycle path alongside the busier Woolwich Road) to return to the river close to the Woolwich Ferry.

4. A 6-mile riverside section follows all the way to Erith. Here you may wish to turn around, catch a train back to Greenwich or carry on along National Cycle Network Route 1 on the banks of the River Darent and River Cray into Dartford.

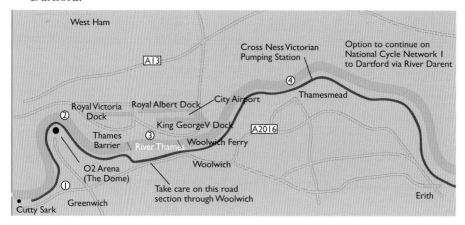